Practice Test #1

Practice Questions

1. Which author of young adult fiction won the Newbery Medal for her novel *A Wrinkle in Time*?
   a. Lois Lowry
   b. J. K. Rowling
   c. Ursula K. Le Guin
   d. Madeleine L'Engle

2. Which of the following works was written closest in time to the literary English Renaissance?
   a. *Beowulf*
   b. *Everyman*
   c. *The Canterbury Tales*
   d. *The Pilgrim's Progress*

3. Which of the following works are members of the same genre? Choose ALL answers that apply.
   a. *King Lear* and *Oedipus Rex*
   b. *Animal Farm* and *Brave New World*
   c. *The Faerie Queene* and *The Gift of the Magi*
   d. *The Open Window* and *For the Union Dead*
   e. *The Waste Land* (Eliot) and *The Waste Lands* (King)

4. Which of the following terms would NOT be used correctly regarding a sonnet?
   a. Sestet
   b. Couplet
   c. Quatrain
   d. Paragraph

5. Among these literary genres, in which pair has one *most* been used within the other?
   a. Nonfiction prose within poetry
   b. Fictional prose within drama
   c. Poetry within fictional drama
   d. Poetry within nonfiction prose

6. The term *soliloquy* is used to refer to an element typically found in which literary genre/subgenre?
   a. Drama
   b. Poetry
   c. Novels
   d. Essays

7. Which pair contains terms typically applied to two subgenres of *two different* literary genres, rather than to two subgenres of the *same single* literary genre?
   a. Picaresque and epistolary
   b. Historical and speculative
   c. Persuasive and expository
   d. Bildungsroman and elegy

8. Among genres of literature, which is typically the most condensed or verbally economical?
   a. A play
   b. A novel
   c. A poem
   d. An essay

9. Of the following titles, which is/are both written in actual essay form AND of essay length, i.e., shorter than book length? Select ALL correct answers.
   a. An Essay on Man
   b. An Essay on Criticism
   c. An Essay on the Shaking Palsy
   d. An Essay on the Principle of Population
   e. An Essay Concerning Human Understanding

10. Which of these elements is LESS likely to be found in drama and in all genres of literature?
    a. Characters
    b. Narrative
    c. Conflict
    d. Action

11. Among the following, which describes a characteristic that the literary genres of satire and realism both share in common?
    a. Ethical issues are often addressed.
    b. Behaviors are often exaggerated.
    c. Language used is straightforward.
    d. Exposure wins over verisimilitude.

12. In comparing and contrasting the sonnet and the ballad as subgenres of the literary genre of poetry, which of these do both forms have in common?
    a. They both have five main kinds.
    b. They both often express love.
    c. They both began with music.
    d. They both have equal meter.

13. What is a primary distinction between the fiction subgenres of historical fiction and science fiction?
    a. One is set in the real past; the other is set in the possible future.
    b. One is based on facts; the other is based on speculations.
    c. One is concerned with events; the other is concerned with inventions.
    d. Answers (a) and (b) both apply; (c) is not necessarily true.

14. Which two subgenres of nonfiction commonly share content type but not authorship type?
    a. Biography and autobiography
    b. Persuasive and informational
    c. Informational and biography
    d. Autobiography and persuasive

The following question is based on the first sentence of Ernest Hemingway's short story

"The Short Happy Life of Francis Macomber" (1936):
> It was now lunch time and they were all sitting under the double green
> fly of the dining tent pretending that nothing had happened.

15. The way Hemingway begins this story gives textual evidence of which literary device?
    a. First-person narrative
    b. *Deus ex machina*
    c. *In medias res*
    d. *Duodecimo*

16. In *Great Expectations,* among relationships involving conflicts that Dickens used to develop the theme of revenge, which choice correctly describes how revenge figured in the relationship?
    a. Miss Havisham takes her revenge against Estella.
    b. Estella takes her revenge against Miss Havisham.
    c. Magwitch takes revenge against protagonist Pip.
    d. Pip takes his revenge against the character Orlick.

17. In the Gilgamesh Epic, the Islamic Quran, and the Old Testament Book of Genesis, which of the following most represents a universal theme they commonly share?
    a. A flood occurring all over the world and destroying everybody
    b. A flood as God's way to eliminate humans behaving wickedly
    c. A flood before which a man is told to build a ship to escape it
    d. A flood after which a survivor sends a bird out to test the flood's end

18. In analyzing the plot structure of a short story, during which part of the plot does the main character experience a turning point?
    a. Exposition
    b. Climax
    c. Rising action
    d. Falling action

19. In Ernest Hemingway's short story, "Hills Like White Elephants" (1927), he describes a conversation between "the girl" (Jig) and "the man" (the American). The dialogue includes this from the girl: "Would you please please please please please please please stop talking." How does this inform the girl's character, the relationship, and the situation? Choose ALL of the correct answers.
    a. It shows she repeats herself a great deal.
    b. It shows the man talks too much for her.
    c. It shows they have discussed this before.
    d. It shows she is frustrated over the topic.
    e. It shows she is not ready for a discussion.

20. In "Old Times on the Mississippi" (1876), Mark Twain writes, "I ... could have hung my hat on my eyes, they stuck out so far." This is an example of which literary device?
    a. Third-person narrative
    b. Personification
    c. Hyperbole
    d. Irony

Answer the following question based on this excerpt from the poem:
"O Captain! My Captain" by Walt Whitman:

O Captain! my Captain! our fearful trip is done,
The ship has weather'd every rack, the prize we sought is won,
The port is near, the bells I hear, the people all exulting,
While follow eyes the steady keel, the vessel grim and daring;
But O heart! heart! heart!
O the bleeding drops of red,
Where on the deck my Captain lies,
Fallen cold and dead.

21. Which of the following poetic devices does Whitman use in this excerpt? Choose ALL correct answers.
　　a. Elegy
　　b. Symbol
　　c. Allusion
　　d. Metaphor
　　e. Apostrophe

22. In which of the following examples has the author created an instance of situational irony?
　　a. In *Great Expectations,* Pip and the readers think Miss Havisham is his benefactor, but it is Magwitch.
　　b. In *The Cask of Amontillado,* Fortunato says a cough won't kill him; Montresor replies, "True—true."
　　c. In *Romeo and Juliet,* Romeo, without the Friar's letter, thinks Juliet is dead; readers know she is alive.
　　d. In every one of these examples, the irony created is dramatic rather than verbal or situational irony.

23. In *The Old Man and the Sea,* Hemingway begins, "He was an old man who fished alone in a skiff in the Gulf Stream and he had gone eighty-four days now without taking a fish." The primary meaning of this opening sentence is
　　a. symbolic
　　b. implied
　　c. literal
　　d. true

Based on the passage below, answer the question that follows.
　　Mamzelle Aurélie had never thought of marrying. She had never been in love. At the age of 20, she had received a proposal, which she had promptly declined, and at the age of 50 she had not yet lived to regret it.

　　(from "Regret" by Kate Chopin)

24. From this passage, which of the following can the reader most accurately infer?
　　a. Mamzelle Aurélie was certainly lonesome.
　　b. Mamzelle Aurélie was quite independent.
　　c. Mamzelle Aurélie was changing her mind.
　　d. Mamzelle Aurélie was sorry to be unwed.

Answer the next three questions based on the following passage:

1. When students miss class, not only do they lose out on important instructional time, but they also miss opportunities to build critical connections with other students and adults. While students are identified as truant when they miss multiple unexcused days of school in a row, students who miss many nonsequential days (excused or unexcused) can fly under the radar. When these absences add up to more or a month or more of school, students are considered "chronically absent."

2. At a national level, an estimated 7.5 million students are considered chronically absent each year. In some states, this translates to 1 in 5 students that do not regularly attend.

3. While missing one or two days of school each month may seem like a nonissue, time away can quickly accumulate and negatively impact mathematics and reading achievement during that school year as well as in the years that follow. For example, chronic absence in kindergarten has a negative impact on academic performance and socioemotional skills, critical building blocks to success.

— Lauren Mims, Fellow, White House Initiative on Educational Excellence, HOMEROOM – official US Department of Education blog, 10/07/2015

25. According to the textual evidence, what differentiates chronic absence from truancy?
    a. The number of school days a student is absent
    b. Whether the absences are excused/unexcused
    c. Sequential versus nonsequential student absence
    d. The excerpt has no textual evidence about this.

26. Where in this passage is there textual evidence supporting the position that chronic absence is a serious issue by citing statistics?
    a. The passage has none.
    b. In the first paragraph
    c. In the second paragraph
    d. In the third paragraph

27. What textual evidence does the author provide to support her statement that missing one or two days of school each month is not the nonissue it seems to be?
    a. Statistics showing the national volume of chronic absences
    b. A generalized example of the negative impacts of absences
    c. None; she simply states it without any supporting evidence.
    d. A differential definition of chronic absences versus truancy

28. In his short story *The Tell-Tale Heart,* Edgar Allan Poe has the main character narrate the tale in the first person. What impact does this have relative to the character's and readers' point of view?
    a. It helps readers to identify with the main character.
    b. It enables readers to sympathize with the narrator.
    c. It lends narrator credibility via a firsthand account.
    d. It emphasizes the character's divorce from reality.

Answer the next two questions based on the following quotation:

> Edward Bulwer-Lytton's 1830 novel *Paul Clifford* opens, "It was a dark and stormy night; the rain fell in torrents—except at occasional intervals, when it was checked by a violent gust of wind which swept up the streets...rattling along the housetops, and fiercely agitating the scanty flame of the lamps that struggled against the darkness."

29. The author's establishment of the setting contributes most to which of the following literary elements?
  a. Plot
  b. Tone
  c. Mood
  d. Conflict

30. In the author's word choices that make this sentence more descriptive, the majority of the arguably most descriptive words are which part of speech?
  a. Verbs
  b. Nouns
  c. Adverbs
  d. Adjectives

Answer the next three questions based on the following poem:

> O Ship of State
> by Henry Wadsworth Longfellow
>
> Thou, too, sail on, O Ship of State!
> Sail on, O Union, strong and great!
> Humanity with all its fears,
> With all the hopes of future years,
> Is hanging breathless on thy fate!
> We know what Master laid thy keel,
> What Workmen wrought thy ribs of steel,
> Who made each mast, and sail, and rope,
> What anvils rang, what hammers beat,
> In what a forge and what a heat
> Were shaped the anchors of thy hope!
> Fear not each sudden sound and shock,
> 'Tis of the wave and not the rock;
> 'Tis but the flapping of the sail,
> And not a rent made by the gale!
> In spite of rock and tempest's roar,
> In spite of false lights on the shore,
> Sail on, nor fear to breast the sea!
> Our hearts, our hopes, are all with thee.
> Our hearts, our hopes, our prayers, our tears,
> Our faith triumphant o'er our fears,
> Are all with thee,—are all with thee!

31. This poem overall is an example of the use of which literary figurative language?
    a. A single metaphor
    b. Extended metaphor
    c. The use of a simile
    d. Use of vivid imagery

32. What is the meter of this poem?
    a. Iambic pentameter
    b. Anapestic tetrameter
    c. Iambic tetrameter
    d. Dactylic dimeter

33. How do the rhyme and meter of this poem contribute to its meaning?
    a. Their regularity reinforces the idea of steady strength.
    b. Their unevenness emphasizes the theme of insecurity.
    c. Their monotony establishes a sense of the unchanging.
    d. Their choppiness mirrors the images of the stormy sea.

34. As a reading strategy, ELA teachers can best give students practice in making predictions to support comprehension through which activity?
    a. Predicting what/whom is a book's subject
    b. Predicting what a novel's character will do
    c. Predicting a significant event in a narrative
    d. Answer (b) and/or (c), not answer (a)

35. Which instructional activity is the best example of the research-based strategy of activating students' prior knowledge before reading?
    a. Before students read a text, the teacher instructs them in relevant background information.
    b. Before and after they read a text, the teacher has students make a KWL chart on its subject.
    c. After students have read a text, the teacher asks them what they know about the subject.
    d. The teacher asks students to express their opinions and reactions on a topic after reading.

36. Regarding literal versus figurative language in informational texts, the words "politician" and "statesman" _____.
    a. have the same denotation and connotation.
    b. have different denotations and connotations.
    c. have the same denotation but different connotations.
    d. have the same connotation but different denotations.

37. Among the Common Core Standards (CCSs) in "anchor" performance skills that all students must demonstrate for reading informational texts, what is required of eleventh and twelfth graders that is NOT required of sixth through tenth graders?
    a. Citing textual evidence to support their inferences and analyses
    b. Identifying specific textual evidence to defend their conclusions
    c. Being able to differentiate strong from weak textual evidence
    d. Being able to recognize which elements are left unclear in a text

38. Students are analyzing the text of Lincoln's *Gettysburg Address*. They are identifying Lincoln's main ideas and details supporting those ideas. Which of the following would be paraphrases of main ideas rather than supporting details? Select ALL correct answers.
    a. Our founding fathers created the United States of America.
    b. The USA was conceived in liberty and is dedicated to equality.
    c. Now the USA is engaged in the great struggle of a civil war.
    d. We are here today to dedicate the Gettysburg battlefield.
    e. It is a fitting and proper thing to commemorate our troops.

39. A teacher helps students analyze informational text to see how authors connect and distinguish ideas by giving them sentence frames, e.g., "_____s are _____, meaning they eat only _____." Students fill these in; e.g., "Rabbits are herbivores, meaning they eat only plants," or "Frogs are carnivores, meaning they eat only meat." These are examples of which of the following:
    a. Making analogies among animals
    b. Grouping animals into categories
    c. Comparing animals by similarities
    d. Contrasting animals' differences

40. Of the following attributes of technical language used in informational texts, which represent(s) the character of the mood rather than the character of the tone?
    a. Concise versus verbose
    b. Impersonal versus personal
    c. Professional versus more familiar
    d. Self-deprecating versus grandiose

41. Shakespeare wrote in Act II, Scene VII of *As You Like It*: "All the world's a stage, /And all the men and women merely players;/They have their exits and their entrances;/And one man in his time plays many parts ...." His meaning here is _____.
    a. primarily denotative
    b. primarily connotative
    c. half one, half the other
    d. neither type of meaning

42. In scientific informational texts, which of these are authors *least* likely to do?
    a. Explicitly state their point of view about the research they did
    b. Explicitly state the purpose of the research they are reporting
    c. Explicitly state their interpretation of the study evidence/data
    d. Explicitly state which variables they investigated and in whom

43. How would an author best use rhetoric to provide readers with supporting evidence of a main point in an informational text?
    a. By evocative descriptions
    b. By making good analogies
    c. By telling personal stories
    d. By reporting case studies

44. A telecommunications salesman is writing informational text to persuade customers to agree to buy the products and services he is selling. One tactic includes advising the customer, "You are hemorrhaging money!" This is an example of using rhetoric to support his purpose through which method of persuasion?
    a. A generalization
    b. Using a metaphor
    c. Rhetorical question
    d. Negative connotation

45. When should scientists use technical rather than nontechnical language to write about technical subjects?
    a. When reporting research results to colleagues in their field
    b. When writing science fiction for a popular reading audience
    c. When writing material to support school science instruction
    d. When writing material to support scientific lobbying efforts

46. Among the following reasons that readers must deduce informational author purposes and motivations for writing, which is most important for identifying purposes an author may have had but did not state in the text?
    a. Determining an author's purpose enables readers to know what to expect from the text.
    b. Discovering the author's motivation for writing allows readers to read for relevant details.
    c. Knowing author motivation and purpose enables critical reader evaluation of author/text.
    d. When authors define purposes that contradict some text, they may have hidden agendas.

47. Regarding the use of rhetoric to support one's purpose, someone may argue, "But if you legalize this drug, all drugs will be legalized." In rhetoric, this is an example of which type of logical fallacy?
    a. Straw man
    b. Red herring
    c. Slippery slope
    d. *Post hoc ergo propter hoc*

48. In an informational text, which of these is most likely to make use of the others?
    a. Irony
    b. Satire
    c. Overstatement
    d. Understatement

49. A word that can modify a verb, an adjective, or an adverb is _____ .
    a. An adjective
    b. An adverb
    c. A noun
    d. A verb

50. The sentence, "After completing the assignment correctly, the teacher gave Peter a high grade" is an example of which kind of error?
    a. A lack of parallelism
    b. A sentence fragment
    c. A dangling participle
    d. A run-on sentence

51. Which version of this sentence is most correctly punctuated and worded?
  a. "Discussing the plan, Maddie and David disagreed, they often had differences of opinion."
  b. "Discussing the plan, Maddie and David disagreed; they often had differences of opinion."
  c. "Discussing the plan, Maddie and David disagreed. They often had differences of opinion."
  d. "Discussing the plan, Maddie and David disagreed; and they often had differences of opinion."

Answer the next two questions based on the sentence below:

> "Although we liked Bill and Hillary, we did not go to their party because there were too many people there for our liking."

52. In the sentence above, what is "Although we liked Bill and Hillary"?
  a. A prepositional phrase
  b. An independent clause
  c. A dependent clause
  d. A complete sentence

53. In the sentence above, which parts are prepositional phrases?
  a. "to their party" and "for our liking"
  b. "Although we liked" and "because there were"
  c. "we did not go" and "because there were"
  d. "because there were" and "too many people"

54. In the words *proactive, progress,* and *projecting, pro-* is a(n) _____ and it means _____.
  a. suffix; good/on top of/over
  b. prefix; before/forward/front
  c. affix; after/behind/in back of
  d. prefix; against/under/below

Answer the next question based on the following sentences:

> "She has made remarkable progress as a student."
> "After a good beginning, her work did not progress."

55. Which can we determine about the word *progress* from context clues in each sentence? Choose ALL correct answers.
  a. It is a noun in the first sentence, with its first syllable stressed.
  b. It is a verb in the first sentence, with its first syllable stressed.
  c. It is a verb in the second sentence, with its second syllable stressed.
  d. It is a noun in the second sentence, with its second syllable stressed.
  e. It is a verb in the first sentence and a noun in the second, and it is pronounced the same.

56. In *Romeo and Juliet,* Shakespeare writes Romeo's line, "What light from yonder window breaks?" What is the syntax of this sentence?
  a. Subject–object–verb
  b. Subject–verb–object
  c. Object–subject–verb
  d. Verb–object–subject

57. A student writing a paper on a topic within a specialized discipline, which she has researched using textbooks published in that field, wants to make sure she has correctly spelled certain words that are part of the terminology particular to that discipline. Which reference should she best consult?

    a. Spell checker
    b. Style manual
    c. Dictionary
    d. Glossary

58. Mark Twain's *The Adventures of Huckleberry Finn* (1885) contains the following quotation of dialogue: "... we's safe! Jump up and crack yo' heels. Dat's de good ole Cairo at las', I jis knows it." Twain was representing the typical dialect of which character?

    a. The uneducated, poor white protagonist, Huck
    b. Huck's best friend, educated white Tom Sawyer
    c. Huck's companion, African-American slave Jim
    d. Jim's (former) owner, wealthy old Miss Watson

59. "This behavior signifies not only a decline in manners, but also common sense." What is a grammatical error in this sentence?

    a. A misplaced modifier
    b. A squinting modifier
    c. A dangling participle
    d. There are no errors.

60. "He woke up, looked at the clock, got dressed, ate a hurried breakfast, got into his car, drove downtown, parked the car, walked across the street and up the block to the corner building next to the grocery store, opened the front door, and went inside." What type of sentence is this?

    a. Compound–complex
    b. Compound sentence
    c. A complex sentence
    d. A simple sentence

61. Which of the following is an example of a complex sentence?

    a. I do not have the time, although I would like to go with you.
    b. I would like to go with you; however, I do not have the time.
    c. I would like to be able to make the time to go out with you.
    d. I'd go, and I'd go with you, if only I could just make the time.

62. "They had planned to be on time; unfortunately, though, unexpected events delayed their arrival." What type of sentence is this?

    a. A simple sentence
    b. Compound sentence
    c. A complex sentence
    d. Compound–complex

63. "After David met Marcia, he knew she was the one, and he soon proposed marriage to her." This is what type of sentence?
   a. It is a compound sentence.
   b. It is a compound–complex sentence.
   c. It is a complex sentence.
   d. It is a simple sentence.

64. "He went to the _____ in order to _____ what happened." By applying knowledge of syntax, which of these could the reader determine?
   a. The parts of speech of the missing words
   b. The specific words for filling in the blanks
   c. The reader can determine neither of these.
   d. The reader could determine both of these.

65. A middle school student notices the vocabulary words *retroactive, retrograde, retrospect, retrospective, retrovirus, retro-rockets,* and *"retro" fashions* in reading school and everyday materials. By knowing the meaning of at least one of these words, the student can determine that the prefix *retro-* means which of the following?
   a. Backward
   b. Forward
   c. Sideways
   d. Upward

66. In a rough draft of an essay, a student has written, "My best friend Gina is a wonderful athlete, a wonderful student, a wonderful person, and a wonderful friend." Which online reference should she consult to improve this description?
   a. A grammar guide
   b. An encyclopedia
   c. A dictionary
   d. A thesaurus

67. In which mode of writing are authors most likely intent on convincing readers to agree with their belief(s) about a given issue?
   a. Narrative
   b. Informative
   c. Explanatory
   d. Argumentative

68. In seven steps, readers can follow for evaluating the argument by an author of persuasive or argumentative writing, what is accurate about the fifth, sixth, and seventh steps?
   a. Authors strengthen their arguments by omitting detracting information.
   b. Authors persuade readers better appealing to emotion than using logic.
   c. Author arguments are valid if reasoning is logical, with sequential points.
   d. Authors can produce credible arguments that are not necessarily valid.

69. If a writer's purpose is to create portraits of people for a reading audience whose interest is in different personalities, motivations, and their expression in various behaviors and relationships, which mode of writing is most appropriate?
  a. A fictional novel
  b. A how-to manual
  c. A persuasive essay
  d. An explanatory paper

70. Which of the following is critically effective for the purposes and audiences of blog writing?
  a. Writing with correct punctuation
  b. Writing with longer paragraphs
  c. Writing with longer sentences
  d. Writing with smaller font size

71. Which two kinds of writing commonly share the characteristic of using subjective, expressive language—among other techniques—to accomplish their purposes with reading audiences?
  a. Speculative and persuasive
  b. Descriptive and speculative
  c. Persuasive and descriptive
  d. Narrative and explanatory

72. To help students select the content and format they will use in writing, what should teachers include in their instruction?
  a. They should have students consider swaying reader opinions more than giving proof.
  b. They should have students consider what readers will agree with instead of disagree with.
  c. They should have students consider not what to impart, but what their readers know.
  d. They should have students consider what information their readers share with them.

73. Regarding organization, what statement is most accurate about outlines relative to writing?
  a. Outlining is only for student writers.
  b. Outlines are for professional writers.
  c. Outlines are for planning, not analyzing.
  d. Outlines aid in planning and analysis.

74. Of the following writing practices, which will interfere with producing a good paragraph?
  a. Confine the content of each paragraph to only one main idea
  b. Develop the main idea in a paragraph by giving specific details
  c. Include a great many supporting details: the more, the better
  d. Use a specific structural pattern to develop each paragraph

75. Which of the following writing techniques that contribute to paragraph coherence is most related to using matching grammatical constructions within, between, and among sentences?
  a. Repetition
  b. Parallelism
  c. Transitions
  d. Consistency

76. When writing an essay, which of the following attributes belongs in the introduction?
   a. Getting the reader's attention
   b. Developing the thesis statement
   c. Giving examples of the thesis idea
   d. Giving the reader a sense of closure

77. What is true about the problem statement in a research paper?
   a. It follows the title of the paper and precedes the abstract.
   b. It tells why the writer cares about the issue s/he identifies.
   c. It cannot be attributed with establishing the paper context.
   d. It will not demonstrate the import of the variables of focus.

78. Which of the following is a primary source?
   a. A report of an original research experiment
   b. An academic textbook's citation of research
   c. A quotation of a researcher in a news article
   d. A website description of another's research

79. When asking a research question, which of these should a researcher do *first*?
   a. Search the literature for knowledge gaps related to the topic.
   b. Search the literature for definitive answers to that question.
   c. Search the literature for additional research needs/openings.
   d. Search the literature for consensus/controversy on the topic.

80. When citing research sources, which of the following must be cited whether the sources are printed or electronic?
   a. Publisher name and publication city
   b. Periodical name, volume, issue, page numbers
   c. Answers (a) and (b) for both print and electronic sources
   d. Database name, database publisher name, URL

81. Of the following statements, which one accurately reflects a principle related to integrating source material into research writing?
   a. Parenthetically naming studies that agree/disagree with one's position interrupts an argument.
   b. If students cannot write an equal/larger number of words about a quotation, it is likely padding.
   c. When quoting sources, students should follow quotations with summaries of what these mean.
   d. Summarizing others' content is as engaging and original as analyses, syntheses, and evaluations.

82. For effectively giving speeches, which attributes are favorable? Choose ALL correct answers.
   a. Formality
   b. Directness
   c. Confidence
   d. Naturalness
   e. Theatricality

83. Which of these accurately reflects influences on media choices for giving presentations?
    a. Combining more than one type of media is advisable.
    b. Experts find it more effective to limit presentations to one medium.
    c. Presenters should not let their budgets be influences.
    d. The length of communication will not affect the media.

84. What is an accurate reflection of criteria for clear, concise speech presentations?
    a. A speaker should not take three or more minutes more to get to the point.
    b. A speaker should not pause before answering audience questions.
    c. A speaker should include as many anecdotes and details as possible.
    d. A speaker should include both necessary and interesting information.

85. Commercials for a mobile service provider frequently reiterate the question, "Can you hear me now?" Which technique of persuasion does this BEST represent?
    a. Repetition
    b. Slogan use
    c. Bandwagon
    d. Testimonial

86. MATCHING: Place the correct number from the right-hand column in the corresponding space next to the choice in the left-hand column.
    a. Meow Mix® ad uses the song "Meow, meow, meow, meow." ___1. Product comparison
    b. The words used lack specific meaning, but they sound good. ___2. Appealing to reason
    c. A brand/product is displayed featuring an American flag. _____3. Appealing to emotion
    d. A checklist contrasts two brands with/without features. _____4. Transfer/association
    e. People are seen enjoying quality time involving a brand. _____5. Glittering generalities
    f. Advertising cites statistics in support of product efficacy. _____6. Appeal via repetition

87. Common Core State Standards for middle school grades include evaluating textual arguments and claims. Within this standard, which of the following is an element applying uniquely to the eighth grade?
    a. Tracing/delineating and evaluating argument and specific claims in a text
    b. Distinguishing claims supported by evidence and reasons versus being unsupported
    c. Assessing whether reasoning is sound and evidence is relevant and sufficient
    d. Recognizing whether some evidence that has been introduced is irrelevant

88. MATCHING: In assessing the soundness of author reasoning, one type of error to look for is a logical fallacy. In the space next to the statement for each letter choice, place the number of the logical fallacy that statement represents.
    a. "Most rapists read pornography as teens; pornography causes rape."   1. Straw man
    b. Of one for strict immigration policy: "He is for killing immigrants."   2. Ad hominem
    c. "Of course she's for affirmative action; she's a minority."   3. Non sequitur
    d. "We need affirmative action because racism is wrong."   4. Post hoc ergo
                                                                     propter hoc

89. Suppose you want to know whether a used car you are looking at is a good vehicle to buy, and the salesperson calls attention to its beautiful paint job. In assessing the relevance of this argument, which of the following applies most?
   a. The paint job is more relevant than the condition of the transmission.
   b. The paint job is less relevant than the fact that the car's frame is bent.
   c. The paint job is more relevant than how well the vehicle's engine runs.
   d. The paint job is less relevant than anything because this is not relevant at all.

90. For supporting language acquisition in English as a second language (ESL)/English language learner (ELL) students, what is most accurate about research-based instructional practices?
   a. Teachers should only state directions verbally to give ELLs English decoding practice.
   b. Teachers should encourage ESL students to respond rapidly to get them up to speed.
   c. Teachers should use idioms without explanations to familiarize ELL students to these expressions.
   d. Teachers should give ELL students models and examples of what they expect in tasks.

91. Research finds that the challenge of assessing learning in ESL student is best met by
   a. Written tests
   b. Oral assessments
   c. Performance assessments
   d. (b) and (c) more likely than (a)

92. To provide accommodations for ELL students, which of these should teachers do in vocabulary and reading instruction?
   a. Teach ELL students vocabulary in isolation.
   b. Teach ELL students vocabulary in context.
   c. Teach ELL students vocabulary in volume.
   d. Teach ELL students reading by their speech levels.

93. Of the following statements, which one is accurate regarding teacher promotion and management of active listening and participation by students in collaborative discussions?
   a. For students inexperienced in group discussions, teachers should use topics below their age levels.
   b. To challenge students, teachers should assign group discussion topics above their age levels.
   c. If teachers explain appropriate discussion behaviors first, modeling them becomes unnecessary.
   d. Teachers should model and explain active listening behaviors for students before discussions.

94. What statement is correct regarding effective teacher techniques for classroom discussions?
   a. When teachers make comments instead of asking questions, it encourages creativity in student responses.
   b. When some students dominate discussion, teachers engage others with more challenging questions.
   c. To meet learning goals, teachers can redirect off-subject discussion by restating topics and questions.
   d. A checklist based on the class attendance roll is not the best way to assess all students' participation.

95. If a student has an assignment to speak before the whole class on a given topic and include a visual aid, which of the following technological tools would be most appropriate?
   a. A PowerPoint presentation
   b. A poster
   c. A blog
   d. A wiki

96. MATCHING: Among free technology tools useful in ELA classes, place the number of the description in the right-hand column in the space next to the matching tool name in the left-hand column.
   a. Edmodo _____
   b. ScreenR _____
   c. YouTube _____
   d. WordPress_____
   e. Google Drive___

   1. A site where teachers can collate screencast videos
   2. A platform enabling students to write and post blogs
   3. An online storage cloud with built-in document tools
   4. A social learning platform for teachers/students/parents
   5. A tool to combine screenshots and voice-overs into videos

97. In differentiated instruction classrooms, which is the most common type of differentiation?
   a. The way individual students access content
   b. The means for assessing the learning goals
   c. The concepts taught to individual students
   d. The amount of detail in teaching concepts

98. How can Lexile measures best help teachers and students choose texts to fit student abilities and interests?
   a. By identifying the grade levels of many books and articles
   b. By finding only texts exactly matching a student's number
   c. By identifying text and student reading levels via numbers
   d. By assigning a number to every book and article published

99. According to research findings, which of these is/are *most* strongly recommended for teaching adolescent reading? Choose ALL correct answers.
   a. Explicit instruction in vocabulary
   b. Explicit comprehension instruction
   c. Extended open discussions of texts
   d. Enhancing student literacy motivation
   e. Enhancing student literacy engagement

100. Relative to the reading comprehension strategy of summarizing text, which one of these is an attribute of a good summary?
   a. A summary is detailed.
   b. A summary is thorough.
   c. A summary has main ideas.
   d. A summary literally repeats the text word for word.

101. Which of the following purposes is/are most applicable to instructional reading strategies and activities conducted *before* students read? Select ALL correct answers.
    a. Constructing graphic organizers
    b. Activating previous knowledge
    c. Determining reading purposes
    d. Writing about and discussing the text
    e. Discussing vocabulary in the text

102. Based on research evidence, what do experts advocate for effectively instructing students in writing strategies?
    a. Teachers should demonstrate strategies and then assign independent student practice.
    b. Teachers should explain strategies and let students practice them without any models.
    c. Teachers should model strategies, then guide practice, then give independent practice.
    d. Teachers should first give students guided practice in strategies and then model them.

103. What do research studies find about student collaboration relative to effective writing instruction?
    a. Cooperative learning does not apply to teaching writing.
    b. Cooperative learning is an effective practice for writing.
    c. Cooperative learning needs no structure from teachers.
    d. Cooperative learning needs structure, not expectations.

104. In writing instruction, what does the process writing approach entail?
    a. Hypothetical audiences for written work
    b. Students work on their own throughout.
    c. Personal responsibility for written work
    d. Writing is evaluated only by the teacher.

105. Which of the following reflects typical characteristics of formative assessments?
    a. They typically use informal methods.
    b. They typically have statistical proof.
    c. They typically are norm referenced.
    d. They typically come after instruction.

106. Relative to formative and summative assessments, research reveals that the single greatest change in classroom instruction for improving student learning and achievement is effective _____, which students and teachers get best from _____ assessments.
    a. comparison; summative
    b. feedback; formative
    c. feedback; summative
    d. comparison; formative

107. Among the following types of tests, which are examples of summative assessments?
    a. Final project critiques
    b. Oral question-and-answer sessions
    c. Running records
    d. Pop quizzes

108. For which of the following purposes would a teacher use a formative assessment?
    a. To get data to inform a school improvement plan
    b. To get or keep government funding for the school
    c. To get data about individual student performance
    d. To get data on student progress over a school year

109. As one approach to gathering student input, what is correct about a K.I.M. chart for learning vocabulary?
    a. The K in K.I.M. stands for know, the I stands for identify, and the M is for meaning.
    b. Under the K in a K.I.M. chart, the student enters the definitions of the word.
    c. Under the K in a K.I.M. chart, the student enters the new vocabulary words.
    d. When students make K.I.M. charts, they never include drawings or pictures.

110. Which of the following methods would give students the most *objective* feedback to enable them to monitor their own performance and progress in speaking and enacting through giving oral reports and presentations?
    a. Having classmates offer peer reviews
    b. Having a teacher evaluate their work
    c. Comparing their work to classmates' work
    d. Viewing videos of their performance

Constructed Response

1. Textual Interpretation: Based on the following excerpt, write a response answering the questions below it.

> I suppose that the high-water mark of my youth in Columbus, Ohio, was the night the bed fell on my father. It makes a better recitation (unless, as some friends of mine have said, one has heard it five or six times) than it does a piece of writing, for it is almost necessary to throw furniture around, shake doors, and bark like a dog, to lend the proper atmosphere and verisimilitude to what is admittedly a somewhat incredible tale. Still, it did take place.
> (From "The Night the Bed Fell" by James Thurber)

What is the author's narrative point of view?
What is the tone of this opening paragraph? How does Thurber establish it? Give examples.
How does the author use foreshadowing? Give examples.

2. Teaching Writing: Read the following example of a seventh-grade student's essay for a descriptive writing assignment with classmates as the target audience. Based on the essay, write a response addressing the three numbered items below it.

> I find plenty of people important in my life. For example, my parents, my big sister and little brother, the kids in my class and my soccer team, and others. One really important person is my best friend Joe.
> I really care about Joe. Joe is always there for me when I need him. When I'm angry about something, he always gets me to smile. When I'm feeling down, he also gets me to smile. I also like Joe because he is interested in the same things I am. For example, playing sports, music videos, and fantasy football.
> Joe sets a good example. He always tells the truth. He has a lot of good qualities. For example, he is cool, he is funny, he is creative, and I can always count on him. I admire him for being independent and not always doing the same things that everybody else does just to fit in.
> My best friend Joe is important to me for a lot of reasons. When I am with him, he makes me feel like I am more important to him than anybody else. He is a true friend.

1. Identify one strength in the student's writing and give examples from the text that illustrate this strength. Do NOT include grammar, punctuation, or other writing conventions.

2. Identify one weakness in the student's writing and give examples from the text that illustrate this weakness. Do NOT include grammar, punctuation, or other writing conventions.

3. Give a description of one follow-up assignment you could give the student who wrote this essay that would either expand upon the strength you identified in #1 OR remediate the weakness you identified in #2. Explain how this assignment would help the student improve his or her writing.

Answers and Explanations

1. **D:** Madeleine L'Engle (1918–2007) won the Newbery Medal for *A Wrinkle in Time* (1963). Lois Lowry (a) (born 1937) won two Newbery Medals for the historical novel *Number the Stars* (1989) and the young-adult dystopian novel *The Giver* (1993). J.K. Rowling (b) (born 1965), best known for her *Harry Potter* series, has won numerous awards, but not the Newbery Medal (she is British; the others are American). Ursula K. Le Guin (c) (born 1929), best known for her *Earthsea* trilogy, has won a great many awards, including a National Book Award for Young People's Literature, but not the Newbery Medal.

2. **D:** *Beowulf* (a), author unknown, is the oldest known epic poem written in Old English, the earliest surviving English literature written in the vernacular, and a major work of Anglo-Saxon literature. It is believed to have been written between c. 975 and 1025, i.e., the Middle Ages (c. 500–1500). *Everyman* (b), author also unknown, is a Christian allegory/morality play written in Middle English in the late 1400s, also during the Medieval period. *The Canterbury Tales* (c) was also written in Middle English, by Geoffrey Chaucer c. 1390—again, in the Middle Ages. *The Pilgrim's Progress* (d), John Bunyan's religious allegory, was published in 1678 during the Tudor period—just after the end of the literary English Renaissance (c. 1500–1670) and before the Enlightenment (c. 1700–1800). Therefore, (d) was written closest in time to literature's English Renaissance.

3. **A and B:** Shakespeare's *King Lear* (c. 1603–1606) and Sophocles' *Oedipus Rex* (c. 495 BCE) are both plays and tragedies (a)—and both are about kings' downfalls. George Orwell's *Animal Farm* (1945) and Aldous Huxley's *Brave New World* (1931) are both dystopian novels (b). *The Faerie Queene* is Edmund Spenser's allegorical epic poem (1590, 1596), *The Gift of the Magi* (c) O. Henry's short story (1905). *The Open Window* is Saki's (1914) short story, and *For the Union Dead* is Robert Lowell's (1964) book of poems (d). Despite similar titles, *The Waste Land* and *The Waste Lands* (E) are different genres: the former is T. S. Eliot's seminal Modernist long poem (1922), and the latter is contemporary author Stephen King's Dark Tower series horror/fantasy/science fiction novel (2003).

4. **D:** A paragraph is a term describing prose, not poetry. All types of sonnets are traditionally 14 lines long. A sestet (a) is a six-line stanza ending Petrarchan/Italian sonnets. Shakespearean sonnets end in a final couplet (b). Spenserian sonnets, which also end in a couplet, have the other 12 lines divided into three quatrains (c) or four-line stanzas.

5. **C:** William Shakespeare's plays are good literary examples of poetry within fictional drama because they are written in verse form. Poems typically do not contain inserted prose (a). Plays are not generally known to incorporate pieces of fictional prose (b). Nonfictional prose sometimes incorporates quotations of poetry or even occasionally original poems, but this occurs much less often than with Shakespeare's plays and many others written entirely or mostly in poetry (d).

6. **A:** A soliloquy is a speech made by one character in a play speaking alone, as opposed to dialogue between/among multiple characters. Some poets (e.g., Robert Browning) have written entire poems in the voice of a single character; however, these are called dramatic monologues rather than soliloquies, a term generally reserved for drama, not poetry (b). Similarly, in novels (c), conversation between/among characters is called dialogue, whereas a long speech by one character would be called a monologue. Essays (d) are typically nonfiction and do not contain characters or their speech.

7. D: A bildungsroman is a term for a novel in which the main character comes of age, develops, learns, and/or grows; an elegy is a term for a poem which mourns the dead. Picaresque refers to a novel about the misadventures of a roguish protagonist; epistolary refers to a novel written in the form of letters/telegrams/other correspondence (a). Fictional novels can be historical, i.e., based on actual events and characters in history, or speculative, i.e., exploring not actual/current/historical but potential/future events/developments (b). Nonfictional essays can be persuasive, i.e., aiming to convince readers of a position, or expository, i.e., aiming to impart information (c).

8. C: Poems are typically the most condensed or economical in their use of words. Plays (a), typically more condensed in language than novels because more of the story is told directly through actions which novels must verbally describe, are still not as condensed as poems because they contain more dialogue. Novels (b) are full-length books, by definition longer than short stories, novelettes, or novellas; they often elaborate more about plot and character development than many poems, thus using more words. They also more often use complete sentences throughout, whereas poems may use phrases in addition to/instead of sentences. Essays (d) tend to expound on nonfictional topics in prose; hence, although they are far shorter than novels, they use many more words to express ideas than plays or most poems.

9. C only: "An Essay on the Shaking Palsy" by James Parkinson, M.D., is an 1817 medical work first defining Parkinson's disease, named after him for identifying it. Its five chapters total fewer than 60 pages. (a) and (b) are both actually long poems by eighteenth-century poet/satirist and essayist Alexander Pope. (d) is a 1798 book by economist Thomas R. Malthus (revised editions 1803–1826). (e) is Enlightenment philosopher John Locke's 1689 (dated 1690) empiricist book in four "books" or sections.

10. B: Characters are always found in drama; they are also found in most fictional short stories and novels, and they are sometimes found in poems. Conflict (c) and action (d) are dramatic elements found not only in plays, but also frequently in short stories, novels, and poetry. Narrative (b) is typically found in novels and short stories; some poems also contain narratives (e.g., Longfellow's *The Song of Hiawatha*, Byron's *Childe Harold's Pilgrimage,* etc.). Although some plays include a narrator who periodically provides summaries, transitions, and/or commentaries, plays generally are LESS likely to contain narrative because the characters' actions tell the story.

11. A: In satire, authors ridicule human failings, including unethical behaviors; in realism, authors often pose ethical dilemmas for their characters to confront and resolve. Behaviors are often exaggerated (b) only in satire, to make fun of and/or attack them; in realism, behaviors are depicted as closely to real-life human behaviors as possible. Straightforward, everyday (vernacular) language used by real, ordinary people is used (c) in realism; in satire, authors may use a variety of language to achieve desired effects of sarcasm, irony, and humor through understatement, overstatement, etc. Exposing human vices and foolishness is more important than accuracy in satire; verisimilitude (representing reality accurately) is more important in realism (d).

12. B: Early ballad themes included jealousy, betrayal, murder, war, famine, poverty, etc. as well as love; early sonnet themes included politics, social standing, satire, etc. as well as love. Both genres have prominently featured expressions of love. The sonnet has five main kinds (a): the Petrarchan/Italian, Occitan, Shakespearean/English, Spenserian, and Modern; the ballad has developed many more variations in form. Originally the ballad was often set to music, and it was later associated with operas and musicals; the sonnet originated in dramatic plays and medieval courts. Though some sonnets have been set to music, the sonnet did not originate with music (c).

The standard ballad meter is iambic heptameter, albeit with variations; the standard sonnet meter is iambic pentameter (d).

13. D: Historical fiction is set during some previous period of our history, which may be remote, recent, or anything in between; science fiction is set during the possible future (a) or during an imagined alternative present—either one with scientific, social, and other developments not part of current reality. Historical fiction is based on periods, events, and facts from history; science fiction is based on speculations (b) of what may occur through extending current science. However, both forms can be concerned with events occurring around and/or to the characters and inventions (real and/or imaginary) could also be included in either one (c).

14. A: Biography and autobiography share a common type of content: the life story of a real person. But they differ in authorship: biography is written by someone other than the subject, whereas autobiography is written about the author's own life. Persuasive and informational (b) nonfiction differ in content: the former seeks to influence readers, and the latter seeks to provide/explain facts objectively. Informational and biographical (c) nonfiction differ in content: the former imparts information about some subject, and the latter imparts information about someone's life. Autobiography tells the writer's life story, whereas persuasive nonfiction seeks to convince readers of something (d).

15. C: Hemingway begins the story in the middle of the action. This literary device is *in medias res,* Latin for "in the middle of things." Its tradition dates to ancient Roman poet Horace's advice to aspiring epic poets not to start with the beginning, but begin with the heart of their story. Textual evidence includes Hemingway's use of "It was now lunch time," implying things had happened before, and "...pretending that nothing had happened," implying something had happened previously. This story does not use first-person narrative (a), e.g., "I/me/we," but third-person narrative ("they," "he," etc.) The quotation does not contain *Deus ex machina* (b), Latin for "God from a machine," i.e., a magical/unbelievable mechanism introduced to resolve a plot conflict. (Its origin is ancient Greek dramas wherein gods intervened onstage, often via elaborate machinery.) *Duodecimo* (d) is a bibliographic book format/size similar to contemporary paperback size (*octavo* is similar to contemporary hardcover book size).

16. B: Miss Havisham uses Estella, not vice versa (a), by raising her to break men's hearts to gain revenge against men for her fiancé having left her at the altar. Estella in turn marries Drummle to get revenge on Miss Havisham (b) for using her. Magwitch uses Pip by raising Pip's social status to get revenge against society, not Pip (c), for discriminating against Magwitch in court on the basis of social class. Orlick wants revenge against Pip, not vice versa (d), for a series of wrongs he feels Pip committed and for Pip's privileged life, which Orlick envies.

17. B: The only choice all three texts share in common is that each religion's god eliminated humans whose behavior had become irredeemably wicked through a great flood. In Genesis, the flood is worldwide (a); the Quran describes the flood as regional (closer to fact according to historians and archeologists identifying a Middle Eastern tidal wave as the source of these narratives). Also, none of these texts describes everybody being destroyed by the flood (a): the Quran says Allah only destroys those who disregard his messengers' communications; the Gilgamesh Epic and Genesis both include survivors. Whereas the Gilgamesh Epic and Genesis each have a man instructed to build a ship to escape the flood (c) and both send birds out to test the flood's end (d), the Quran does not include an ark/ship or birds.

18. B: The parts of plot structure are exposition, rising action, climax, falling action, and dénouement or resolution. In the exposition (a), the setting is established, characters introduced, and plot background presented. During the rising action (c), the story builds up to the chief conflict or problem. During the climax (b) or crisis, the high point of the story, the main character's challenge reaches a peak; then a turning point occurs that determines the outcome. During the falling action (d), the story slows down as outcomes of the character's decisions/actions are revealed. During the dénouement or resolution, the author ties up loose ends, and the story is concluded with an unhappy or happy ending.

19. C and D: The girl's repetition of "please" seven times, in the context of the dialogue, shows the couple has had this conversation many times (c) and that she is frustrated over this (d). Hemingway does not use repetition to show the character repeats herself a lot (a) or the man talks too much (b), but to show that after numerous inconclusive discussions, she explodes. Earlier in the same dialogue, she has said, "Can't we maybe stop talking?" The dialogue shows she is not unready to talk (e), but she is sick of talking without resolution. Hemingway sets the story at a railway station crossroads, symbolizing the girl's decisions about her situation and the relationship also at a crossroads.

20. C: This is an example of hyperbole, i.e., extreme exaggeration to create an effect. In this case, the effect is humor. Twain describes his reaction: "I was helpless. I did not know what in the world to do. I was quaking from head to foot..." and then he elaborates on this description by saying his eyes protruded so far he could have hung his hat on them, which is obviously not literally possible. This is an eighteenth-century verbal precursor of twentieth-century cartoon graphics in which a character's eyes bug out unnaturally far to indicate an extreme reaction. This is not an example of third-person narrative (a); it is first-person narrative. It is not personification (b), i.e., attributing human qualities/actions to inanimate objects or animals. It is not irony (d), which creates humor, sarcasm, satire, or sadness through stating something in terms opposite to its meaning.

21. A, B, C, D, and E: Whitman managed to use all of these devices in his poem, and even in this single excerpted stanza. The poem is an elegy (a) on the death of Abraham Lincoln. Whitman uses the heart as a symbol (b) of his grief over the loss of President Lincoln. Whitman makes allusions (c) to the Union's victory in the Civil War, and to Lincoln's death. The entire poem uses an extended metaphor (d) wherein the ship is the United States, the "fearful trip" is the Civil War, and Lincoln is the ship's captain. When he addresses Lincoln directly, "O Captain! my Captain!" even though he is not there, Whitman uses apostrophe (e), i.e., naming and speaking directly to a real or imagined listener or thing.

22. A: In situational irony, things are revealed as other than they seem to both characters and readers, such as when Dickens makes Miss Havisham appear to be Pip's benefactor, only to reveal ultimately that it is really Magwitch. In verbal irony, a character (or narrator) says one thing but means another, such as when Poe has Montresor agree with Fortunato's literal statement that he will not die of a cough; ultimately, readers discover Montresor's true meaning: the cough will not kill Fortunato because Montresor will (b). In dramatic irony, a character knows less than the readers/audience, like Romeo (c). Therefore, (d) is incorrect.

23. C: The meaning of this opening sentence is primarily literal: it establishes who the main character is, what he does, and his current situation. While this novella contains some symbols, the opening sentence is not symbolic (a) of anything particular. The meaning is not implicit (b) but explicit. (Hemingway was known for the clear, direct simplicity of his writing style.) The sentence is not true (d) because this book is a work of fiction.

24. B: The reader can infer that Mamzelle Aurélie was independent from the description of her never having thought of marrying, never having been in love, having declined a proposal, and so far never having lived to regret this. Readers cannot infer *from this passage alone* that she was lonesome (a), was changing her mind (c), or was sorry she was unmarried (d). Readers may infer from the *title* she ultimately regrets something in this story, but not from this passage alone.

25. C: According to the first paragraph, it is not a certain number of absences (a)—no numbers are identified there—that distinguishes chronic absence from truancy. Whereas truancy is defined as many sequential days of unexcused absences, chronic absence is defined as nonsequential days of excused OR unexcused absences, so whether they are excused or not does not differentiate chronic absence from truancy (b). The difference is defined as sequential versus nonsequential absence days (c); therefore, (d) is incorrect.

26. C: The second paragraph cites a national statistic of the estimated annual number of chronically absent students; plus it offers a statistic of the proportion this represents for some states. Therefore, (a) is incorrect. The first paragraph (b) identifies academic and social benefits students miss through absence, and differentially defines truancy versus chronic absence, but it does not cite any statistics. The third paragraph (d) gives general examples of the impacts of chronic absence, but it gives no supporting statistics.

27. B: The statistics (a) given in the second paragraph do not support the statement referenced; they precede it, supporting the first paragraph's definition of chronic absence and its reality in numbers. The author supports her statement in the third paragraph's opening sentence by following with a generalized example of how cumulative absences negatively affect current and future student achievement and success. Therefore, (c) is incorrect. The differential definition (d) given in the first paragraph establishes what chronic absence is; it does not support the third paragraph's statement.

28. D: By having the main character narrate in the first person, Poe emphasizes his divorce from reality: he repeatedly insists he is not crazy, simultaneously demonstrating he is by describing his abnormal obsession, paranoid delusions, oblivion to normal cues like noises that would alert neighbors, and gloating over his brilliance in committing the perfect crime even though he has already betrayed his guilt to police. Readers do not identify with (a) or feel more sympathetic (b) toward him; if anything, they feel more detached from him through his speaking for himself than if a sane, third-person narrator told his story. His firsthand account does not lend him credibility (c): Poe deliberately uses the first-person narrative point of view to illuminate the character's madness through his speech.

29. C: Though the first clause of this sentence has been widely maligned, ridiculed, parodied and praised, imitated, and even made the basis of literary contests for both bad and good writing, it and the rest of the sentence do establish the setting such that it contributes greatly to mood, i.e., the emotions it evokes in readers. It does not contribute to plot (a) because it includes no actions or events yet. It does not contribute to tone (b), which reflects the attitude of the author rather than evoking an attitude in the reader. It does not contribute to conflict (d) in the same way it does not contribute to plot.

30. D: The arguably most descriptive words in this sentence are adjectives: dark, stormy, violent, scanty. Bulwer-Lytton also used verbs (a), i.e., fell, was checked, swept, rattling, agitating, struggled; although the last four of these are descriptive, they are arguably not as descriptive as the adjectives.

- 27 -

He used some descriptive nouns (b) as well: night, rain, gust, wind, darkness; yet these are still not as evocative as the adjectives. Of adverbs (c), "fiercely" is certainly descriptive, but it is the only one.

31. B: This poem is a classic example of extended metaphor, an implied comparison that extends across the entire work, here of America's Union ("state") as being like a sailing ship braving the treacherous waters of governance. A single metaphor (a) is an isolated incidence of such an implied comparison within a work rather than one encompassing the whole work. A simile (c) is a direct/explicit comparison, e.g., "The state is *like* a ship." The poem does contain auditory, visual, and tactile imagery (d), but extended metaphor is the most prominent literary device of the poem overall.

32. C: This poem is written in iambic (∪ / = one unstressed syllable, then one stressed) tetrameter (four beats per line). Iambic pentameter (a), with five iambic beats per line, is the most common meter in English verse; all of Shakespeare's verses use it. A specific example is Theodore Roethke's villanelle, "The Waking." An example of anapestic (∪∪ / = two unstressed syllables, then one stressed) tetrameter (b) is George Gordon, Lord Byron's "The Destruction of Sennacherib." Dactylic (/∪∪ = one stressed, two unstressed syllables) dimeter (two beats per line) (d) is used by Alfred, Lord Tennyson in "The Charge of the Light Brigade."

33. A: The very regular rhyme and meter in this poem reinforce the idea of the ship of state as strong and forging steadily onward despite all perils. Therefore, these are not uneven, and the poem does not have a theme of insecurity (b). Though regular, the rhyme and meter are not monotonous, and Longfellow meant to convey a sense that the ship of state was steadfast, brave, and dependable/worthy of the people's faith and hope, not unchanging (c). The regular rhyme and meter are even, not choppy; although Longfellow describes a stormy sea as part of the extended metaphor, he does not mirror it in sound or rhythm (d).

34. D: Predicting what (e.g., a quest or a war) or whom (e.g., a prince or three animals) a book is about (a) is a common practice of students who fall back on the easiest answer to a teacher's request to make predictions. It is more useful for teachers to challenge students to try and predict what a character in a novel will do (b) or a significant event that may occur in a story (c). Teachers can explain to students that they can do "detective" work to make predictions by looking for clues in book titles, front-cover illustrations, and illustrations inside a book before even reading it. They can also have students read just one passage from a book, and then have them predict what will occur next.

35. B: A KWL chart has students list before reading what they know about a subject; what they want to know/learn about it; and after reading, what they have learned about it. This is a good example of a research-based instructional strategy for activating students' prior knowledge. Answer (a) is not a good example because the teacher gives the students background information rather than finding out what they already know. Answer (c) is not a good example because the teacher asks students what they know about the subject AFTER they have read a text, not BEFORE. Activating prior knowledge BEFORE reading enables students to build upon what they already know when they begin reading, as successful readers do, versus beginning to read without thinking, as less successful readers do. Similarly, the teacher should ask students their opinions and reactions about a topic BEFORE they read, not after (d), to activate their existing knowledge

36. C: Denotation is the literal meaning or dictionary definition of a word. Connotation is the figurative meaning of a word, including emotional or perceptual associations associated with the word but not included in its literal definition. The words "politician" and "statesman" have the same

literal meaning or denotation. However, when used in context, "politician" may have either a neutral or negative connotation, whereas "statesman" usually has a positive connotation.

37. D: Common Core Standards for the English Language Arts require "anchor" performance skills for citing textual evidence to support their inferences and analyses (a) of sixth graders. They require seventh graders to do this and also to identify several specific pieces of textual evidence to defend their conclusions (b). They require eighth graders to do both of these plus be able to differentiate stronger from weaker textual evidence (c). They require all these, plus citing strong and thorough textual evidence, of ninth and tenth graders. They require eleventh and twelfth graders to do all of the aforementioned and be able to identify which elements in a text are left unclear (d).

38. A, C, and D: Lincoln's statement that our founding fathers created the USA is a main idea. That it was "... conceived in liberty, and dedicated to the proposition that all men are created equal" (b) represent details supporting the main idea of (a). His statement that "Now we are engaged in a great civil war" (c) is another main idea. A supporting detail is that this war is "testing whether that nation, or any nation so conceived and so dedicated, can long endure." His statement that "We have come to dedicate a portion of that field ..." is another main idea (d). Details supporting the latter main idea include that this field is "... a final resting place for those who here gave their lives that that nation might live"; and "It is altogether fitting and proper that we should do this" (e).

39. B: These are examples of grouping animals into categories. Authors connect and distinguish ideas and things in informational texts by making analogies (a). e.g., a frog is to an insect as a lion is to an antelope—i.e., predator to prey. Authors can also group them into categories, as is done here. Some authors compare their similarities (c) and/or contrast their differences (d), e.g., some animals have simple life cycles; some, such as frogs, undergo metamorphosis; and some insects undergo complete metamorphosis including egg, larval, pupal, and adult stages, whereas other insects, such as grasshoppers, dragonflies, and cockroaches, undergo incomplete metamorphosis with egg, nymph, and adult stages but no pupal stage.

40. D: Writers of technical language, as in scientific informational texts, need to find a balance between seeming too self-deprecating or too grandiose. For example, "Our findings will change the world" is grandiose, whereas "Our findings are insignificant" is self-deprecating. "Our results are promising and indicate the need for further research" is more balanced. These are examples of the mood of the language. Technical language should be concise (a) by not using superfluous words, impersonal (b) and detached by using passive voice and avoiding overuse of the first person and the vernacular, and professional (c) by using more technical terminology rather than more familiar everyday vocabulary. These are examples of the tone of the language.

41. B: Shakespeare used the connotative meanings of the words to create a metaphor, wherein the stage, players, exits and entrances, and parts played symbolize the world, people, and roles or stages in life. Therefore, his meaning is NOT primarily denotative (a), i.e., focusing on the literal word definitions; nor is it half denotative and half connotative (c). The words must have one or the other type of meaning, not neither (d): text authors use words literally or figuratively or both.

42. A: Authors of scientific informational text, such as research study reports, are likely to state the purpose of their research (b). They are likely to state their interpretations of the evidence or data their study produced (c). And in any acceptable research report, they will always identify which variables they studied, the population in whom they studied them (d), the number of the sample size, the conditions of the experiment, and the research methodology used. However, they are *least*

likely to explicitly state their point of view about their research (a), unlike authors of other types of informational text who directly state their viewpoint about the topic and/or their reason(s) for writing about it.

43. D: Reporting case studies is the best example of using rhetoric to provide supporting evidence of an author's main point in an informational text. Writing evocative descriptions (a) is an example of using rhetoric to appeal to the reader's emotions in an informational text, not to provide supporting evidence. Making good analogies (b) is an example of using rhetoric to illustrate and/or illuminate the author's point(s) rather than actually supporting them with evidence. Telling personal anecdotes (c) is an example of using rhetoric to give readers examples that are more accessible and realistic to illustrate their points, not to provide evidence supporting them.

44. B: This is an example of a metaphor. The literal meaning of hemorrhaging is copious bleeding. In this example, it is used figuratively in a metaphor for losing money at a volume and rate comparable to severe blood loss denoted by hemorrhage. It is not a generalization (a). An example of using a generalization persuasively is "We all want peace, not war." It is not a rhetorical question (c) or a question at all. An example of using a rhetorical question (needing no answer) persuasively is "Wouldn't you rather get paid more than less?" The example is not of negative connotation (d), because the word "hemorrhage" already has a negative denotation—i.e., the literal meaning of hemorrhaging is never a good thing. An example of using negative word connotation persuasively is, "You could stay with this *expensive* plan..." followed by contrasting positive connotation: "... or choose the *money-saving* plan I'm offering."

45. A: Scientists should use technical language to write about technical subjects when they are reporting research results to colleagues in their field, who will understand it. However, scientists who also write science fiction (b) will need to write in nontechnical language for the popular reading audience to understand it. When scientists write material to support school instruction in the sciences (c), they must also use nontechnical language for students and teachers to understand it. And when they write material to support scientific lobbying efforts (d), they must use nontechnical language for the politicians who hear/read it to understand the messages they are communicating and the appeals they are making for legislation and/or funding.

46. D: One way a reader can determine that an informational text author may have had a hidden agenda is if the author's stated purposes for writing contradict other parts of the text. When the reader can identify motivations the author has not stated, the reader is better able to evaluate how effective the text is and whether they agree or disagree with it, and why. It is equally true that knowing the author's purpose enables readers to know what to expect from text (a) that knowing author motivation helps with reading for relevant details (b) and that knowing authors' purposes and motivations facilitates critical reader evaluation of the author and text (c). However, (d) is most related to the importance of discovering unstated author purposes for evaluating text.

47. C: This is an example of a slippery slope argument that is a logical fallacy. The fallacious form of the slippery slope is essentially a non sequitur; i.e., it argues that one thing will cause other things without showing any cause-and-effect relationship between them. A straw man (a) argument is a logical fallacy that, instead of refuting someone else's actual argument, refutes an exaggeration or caricature of it. A red herring (b) is a piece of irrelevant information introduced to distract attention from the real issue. *Post hoc ergo propter hoc* (d) is Latin for "after this, therefore because of this." It means arguing that one thing was caused by another that happened before it. This is a logical fallacy because, like correlation, chronological order does not equal causation.

48. B: Satire is a genre of writing that may be used in informational as well as literary (and informational literary) texts to ridicule human and social faults through various indirect devices, including irony (a), i.e., saying the opposite of what one means; overstatement (c), i.e., exaggerating; and/or understatement (d), i.e., minimizing the importance or seriousness of something in describing it.

49. B: Adjectives (a) modify nouns or pronouns by describing them, e.g., *white* is an adjective describing and modifying the noun *house.* Adverbs (b) modify verbs, adjectives, or other adverbs—everything *except* nouns or pronouns. Adverbs answer the questions *how, when,* or *where,* e.g., *slowly, later,* or *downstairs.* Nouns (c) are words that name a person, place, or thing, e.g., *girl, city,* or *house.* They do not modify other parts of speech. They are typically subjects or objects in sentences, clauses, or phrases. Verbs (d) identify actions or states of being, e.g., *to run, to smile, to feel,* or *to be.* Like verbs, they do not modify other words. They are typically predicates in sentences, clauses, or phrases. *To be* can also be a linking verb (copula).

50. C: This is an example of a dangling participle. The participle *completing* was done by Peter, but the sentence construction makes it seem as if the teacher did it. This makes no sense: the teacher would not give Peter a high grade after completing the assignment correctly. It can be corrected to "After Peter completed the assignment correctly, the teacher gave him a high grade" or "After completing the assignment correctly, Peter received a high grade from the teacher."

51. B: A semicolon is used to punctuate between two independent clauses, as in the sentence given. It is also used in sentences that contain additional internal punctuation, which this sentence also has. (a) is incorrect because it contains a comma splice, i.e., two independent clauses joined by a comma without a coordinating conjunction (such as "and" or "but"). (c) is not as correct because it separates two related clauses with a period; joining them with a semicolon reinforces their connection. Choice (d) incorrectly uses a semicolon together with the coordinating conjunction "and." With a coordinating conjunction between independent clauses, a comma should be used rather than a semicolon.

52. C: "Although we liked Bill and Hillary" is a dependent clause. It is a clause because it has a subject, "we," and a verb, "liked." It is dependent or subordinate because it begins with a subordinating conjunction, "although." So it cannot stand alone as an independent clause (b), but it depends on and modifies the independent clause "we did not go (to their party)." It is not a prepositional phrase (a) because it does not begin with a preposition. It is not a complete sentence (d) because it is not an independent clause.

53. A: "To their party" and "for our liking" are prepositional phrases because they begin with the prepositions "to" and "for," respectively. The first phrase modifies the predicate (verb) "go"; the second phrase modifies the dependent clause "because there were (too many people there)": "for" is the preposition; the pronoun "our liking" is the object of the preposition. "Although we liked ..." and "because there were ..." (b) are both dependent clauses. "We did not go" (c) is an independent clause. "Too many people" is an adverbial phrase modifying the verb "were": "too" is an adverb modifying the adjective "many," which modifies the noun "people" (d).

54. B: The prefix *pro-* from Latin means before, earlier, prior to; for, forward; or front. Prefixes come at the beginnings of words. Suffixes come at the ends of words, and *pro-* does not mean good, on top of, or over (a). The Greek prefix *eu-* means good; the Latin prefix *supra-* means above, and the Latin prefix *super-* can mean over and above, among other meanings. Prefixes and suffixes are both affixes (c); however, *pro-* does not mean after/behind/in back of. The Latin prefix *post-* means after

or behind; *retro-* means back or backward. *Pro-* does not mean against/under/below (d). *Sub-* means under or below; *anti-* means against.

55. A and C: We can tell from the context that in the first sentence, *progress* is a noun because it is the object of the verb "has made" and is modified by the adjective "remarkable." The object of the verb cannot be another verb, and adjectives modify nouns, not verbs. The noun "progress" is pronounced with the first syllable stressed. From the context, we can tell that in the second sentence, *progress* is a verb because it modifies the noun subject "work." Nouns do not modify other nouns, and the subject needs a verb. The verb *progress* is pronounced with the second syllable stressed.

56. A: "Light" is the subject of the sentence; "from yonder window" is a prepositional phrase beginning with the preposition "from," then the adjective "yonder," modifying the object "window," an indirect object modifying the verb, "breaks." Subject–verb–object (b) is the typical syntax of most English sentences; Shakespeare changes this by placing the verb at the end of the sentence instead of after the subject and before the object as is most common. Answer (c) would be "From yonder window what light breaks?" Answer (d) would be "Breaks from yonder window what light?"

57. D: She should use the glossaries in the textbooks that were her research sources. Glossaries are alphabetized lists of vocabulary/terminology used in the text with their definitions. These will give correct spellings; she can also use the definitions to ensure correct spelling among very similar words. She should not use the spell checker (a) of her computer's word processing software program: these typically do not recognize specialized, discipline-specific terminology/vocabulary. She should not use a style manual (b), which is only to find the correct format for papers and citing references in a particular style (MLA, APA, Turabian, etc.). She should not necessarily use a dictionary (c) before the glossaries in her reference texts: although many good dictionaries include specialized terminology/vocabulary words, they may not include them all.

58. C: This quotation is dialogue spoken by Jim, the African-American slave. Twain was representing the typical dialect of an uneducated slave in the American South of the nineteenth century. Twain used a distinctly different dialect for the dialogue spoken by Huck, who is also uneducated and poor but white (a). Huck's friend Tom Sawyer also speaks with the casualness of youth and in a Southern regional white dialect, but his dialogue, reflecting more education, is less ungrammatical and contains fewer folk expressions than Huck's (b). Miss Watson also speaks like a nineteenth-century Southerner, but in contrast, her speech reflects the refined, formal qualities of more extensive education, wealth, and age (d).

59. A: This sentence contains a misplaced modifier: "not only" modifies "a decline," and "but also" modifies "common sense." This is illogical because "not only" and "but also" are logically connected and thus should both modify the objects of the preposition "in," which in turn modify the noun "decline." To be correct, it should be written either as "not only a decline in manners, but also a decline in common sense" or as "a decline not only in manners, but also in common sense." This is not a squinting modifier (b), which makes the meaning unclear by potentially modifying either of two words, e.g., "Children who smile seldom are sad," which could mean children who rarely smile are sad, or children who smile are rarely sad. It is not a dangling participle (c), e.g., "While growing up, Popsicles were popular," wherein the participle is left dangling without a subject: the Popsicles were not growing up. It should be something like, "While growing up, we liked Popsicles" or "While I was growing up, Popsicles were popular." Because (a) is correct, (d) is incorrect.

60. D: This is a simple sentence despite its length. It has only one independent clause, which contains a single subject (He) and a compound predicate with multiple verbs (woke, looked, got, ate, got, drove, parked, walked, opened, went). All other parts are prepositions, prepositional phrases, adjectives, adverbs, and articles modifying verbs and nouns. The other types all include more than one clause—either more than one independent plus at least one dependent clause (a), more than one independent clause (b), or an independent and a dependent clause (c).

61. A: A complex sentence combines independent and dependent clauses. The first clause is independent, the second ("although...") is dependent as it cannot stand alone as a sentence. Choice (b) is a compound sentence, i.e., two independent clauses joined by a coordinating conjunction. Choice (c) is a simple sentence, i.e., a single independent clause. Choice (d) is a compound–complex sentence, i.e., two independent clauses joined by coordinating conjunction ("and"), followed by a dependent ("if ...") clause.

62. B: This is a compound sentence, i.e., two independent clauses joined by a conjunctive adverb ("unfortunately"). It is not a simple sentence (a) because it has two independent clauses; a simple sentence would have only one. It is not a complex sentence (c) because it has no dependent clauses; a complex sentence has at least one independent and one dependent clause. It is not a compound–complex (d) sentence because it has no dependent clause; a compound–complex sentence has at least two independent clauses and at least one dependent clause.

63. B: This is a compound–complex sentence because it includes a dependent clause ("After David met Marcia"), which cannot stand on its own as a sentence but depends on an independent clause, plus two independent clauses ("he knew she was the one" and "he soon proposed marriage to her") joined by a coordinating conjunction ("and"). A compound sentence (a) has two independent clauses but no dependent clause. A complex sentence (c) has at least one dependent clause and only one independent clause, not two. A simple sentence (d) has only one independent clause and no dependent clauses.

64. A: From the syntax of this sentence, the reader can determine which parts of speech the missing words must be: the first blank must be filled by a noun, the second by a verb. However, the reader cannot determine from syntax which specific noun or verb these should be (b). The noun must be a thing, place, or event, but this encompasses a great many words (e.g., building, site, meeting, party, riot, class, school, company, etc.). The verb must be transitive because it takes an object ("what happened"), but this also includes myriad verbs (e.g., see, observe, find out, discover, report, address, change, correct, imitate, avoid, etc.). Therefore, answers (c) and (d) are incorrect.

65. A: *Retro-* is Latin meaning backward or behind. Retroactive means acting backward, i.e., upon earlier events (e.g., "Monthly fees will be refunded retroactively to your first payment"). Retrograde refers to moving backward, e.g., planets in astronomy; deteriorating/degenerating in biology, or generally in reverse order or receding. Retrospect/retrospective mean looking backward on previous events. A retrovirus (e.g., the AIDS virus) enables reversing genetic transcription to be RNA-to-DNA to produce new RNA retroviruses by incorporating viral DNA into the host's DNA, instead of typical DNA-to-RNA transcription. Retro-rockets decelerate or separate stages of larger rockets to which they are attached by aiming exhaust toward instead of away from flight direction, i.e., backward. "Retro" fashions are inspired by earlier styles. By knowing the meaning of at least one of these words, the student can determine the meaning of the prefix, and thus of the other words.

66. D: The student has used the same adjective, "wonderful," four times in the same sentence to modify four different nouns. To give her description more variety, she should consult an online thesaurus to find synonyms (e.g., terrific, great, outstanding, exemplary, etc.). A grammar guide (a) will not offer vocabulary synonyms, and the student's sentence has no grammatical issues. An encyclopedia (b) offers information on many subjects, but not word synonyms. An online dictionary (c) will provide a few to several synonyms for "wonderful," but a thesaurus will offer many more.

67. D: The argumentative mode of writing has the purpose of convincing readers to agree with the author's belief or opinion about a chosen issue. The narrative (a) mode has the purpose of telling readers a story. The telling may include sharing an insight or revelation that the author or character(s) gained through the story's experiences and/or something they learned through them. The informative (b) mode has the purpose of sharing information with readers, to tell them something they did not know, and/or how to do something. The explanatory (c) mode shares information with readers and also analyzes, illuminates, or illustrates it for the purpose of helping them understand it.

68. C: In the fifth of seven reader steps for evaluating argumentative writing, readers assess whether the author's argument is complete. Some authors may not present enough supporting evidence, or they may omit information that detracts from their argument, making their argument incomplete (a) rather than including such detracting material and then refuting it, which makes the argument more complete. The reader's sixth step is to determine the validity of the author's argument. Although argumentation may sway reader opinion by influencing reader feelings, valid arguments also use clear, logical reasoning rather than relying solely upon emotional appeals (b); the points they make follow a sequence, with one leading to the next (c). The seventh reader step is to decide if the argument is credible. For an argument to be believable, it must first be valid; hence, (d) is incorrect.

69. A: A fictional novel is a form of narrative writing, which tells a story. In addition to plot and setting, characters are key elements of narrative. In developing characters, authors depict their personality characteristics, mannerisms, behaviors, and interactions with other characters for audiences interested in personalities, motivations, and relationships in stories. A how-to manual (b) is informational writing. The author's purpose is informing how to do something by giving sequential steps, diagrams, and/or descriptions of the order and/or manner in which it should be done, for readers seeking specific instructions in how to complete a process or task. The writer of a persuasive essay (c) has the purpose of convincing readers to agree with a point or argument. The audience is interested in the issue being argued. The writer of an explanatory paper (d) would seek to clarify facts, ideas, or processes for an audience seeking to understand these.

70. A: Bloggers need to use correct punctuation to encourage continued reading of their posts. If they are not already confident in their grasp of punctuation, they should write in shorter sentences (c) until they are confident. Because reading on computer screens is harder than on paper, paragraphs in blogs must be significantly shorter than in print, not longer (b). Shorter paragraphs enable readers to "chunk" the information. Font sizes should be larger rather than smaller (d) to be easier on readers' eyes and more legible on screen.

71. C: Persuasive or argumentative writing uses a combination of logic; proof; supporting evidence; and subjective, expressive language to influence reader feelings and beliefs. Descriptive writing also appeals to reader emotions, as well as reader imaginations and senses, by vividly portraying sensory details to recreate experiences, events, and scenes so that readers feel they are also experiencing what is described. Speculative writing does not aim to convince readers as persuasive

writing does (a). It does not aim to recreate experiences for readers as descriptive writing does (b). Rather, speculative writing invites readers to explore diverse ideas and their potential outcomes. As such, it uses looser structure and less definitive points than persuasive or expository writing. Narrative writing aims primarily to tell a story. This may include affecting reader feelings through subjective, expressive language. However, explanatory (d) writing does not share this characteristic; it aims to inform readers and explain information to them.

72. D: For writing, teachers should instruct their students to think about what kinds of proof and/or evidence they will need to provide for their readers to agree with their points (a). They should instruct students to consider not only what points they will make in writing that their readers might agree with, but moreover what points their readers are likely to disagree with (b), and how to refute or counter those disagreements to persuade skeptical audiences. Teachers should have students think about what information their readers already know and what information they will share with their readers (c). They should additionally instruct students to consider what information they and their readers share in common (d).

73. D: Outlines benefit students (a) and professional writers (b), not only one or the other. The main point(s) of a paragraph or an entire piece, and the details that support the main point(s), can be more quickly identified in outlines that summarize them in single sentences than they can by reading through all the additional language of a fully developed piece. Outlines can be used not only to plan writing (c), but also to analyze existing writing (d). Readers (or writers reviewing their own work) can make outlines to summarize the main point/idea in one sentence, and then list and number the supporting details, also each in a single sentence.

74. C: Focusing each paragraph on one main idea (a) contributes to writing good paragraphs. The writer may state this idea overtly in a topic sentence, or simply imply a more obvious main topic that readers can infer. Giving specific details to develop that main idea (b) is also a practice that results in better paragraphs. However, it is not true that the more details, the better (c): excessive details will destroy the paragraph's focus and confuse readers. Another practice for developing good paragraphs is using specific structural patterns (d), e.g., comparison–contrast, division and classification, analogy, cause-and-effect, definition, description, narration, process, or example and illustration.

75. B: Parallelism refers to parallel structure, i.e., maintaining the same grammatical construction among like and related words or phrases. For example, "He likes to hike, climb mountains, and ride bicycles" uses parallelism by keeping all of the verbs in the infinitive; "He likes to hike, climb mountains, and riding bicycles" lacks parallelism because the first two verbs are infinitives but the third is a participle/gerund. Repetition (a) lends coherence by connecting a paragraph's sentence through repeating its important words, phrases, and their referents (e.g., pronouns). Transitions (c) give coherence by using words and phrases to connect sentences to one another. Consistency (d) provides coherence by maintaining the same tone, point of view, and language register throughout the paragraph and the whole piece.

76. A: The introduction of an essay should get the reader's attention; engage the reader's interest; state and integrate the main thesis within it; and give an overview of the essay's organization or structure, e.g., by summarizing the main point and supporting evidence. Developing the thesis statement (b) and giving examples of the idea in the thesis (c) belong in the body of the essay. Giving the reader a sense of closure (d) belongs in the conclusion of the essay.

77. B: In a research paper, the problem statement follows the title and the abstract; it does not come before the abstract (a). It identifies the issue under study and explains why this issue is important to the writer (b). It also does establish the context for the body of the paper (c). In addition, the problem statement defines the scope of the research being reported by identifying the specific variables of focus in the research, and it does show what is important about these variables (d).

78. A: When a researcher has conducted an original experiment and reports the results, findings, and associated conclusions in a research report, that report is considered a primary source. Academic textbooks, journal articles, articles in other periodicals, and authoritative databases may all be primary sources. When an academic textbook cites research (b) by others, that citation is considered a secondary source because it refers to information originally presented by others. When a news article quotes a researcher's writing (c), that is also a secondary source and so is a description given on a website of another person's research (d).

79. B: The first thing a researcher should look for in a review of the existing literature related to a specific research question is whether that question has already been definitively answered. If so, the researcher should ask a different research question. If the question has not already been answered conclusively, then the researcher can look for gaps in knowledge about the topic that searching the literature reveals (a). S/he can review the literature to find what needs and opportunities for further research other researchers have identified (c). The researcher can also examine the literature to discern whether there is consensus, controversy, or both and if so, what those opinions are about the topic (d). These considerations help inform the direction for research.

80. C: Publisher name and publication city (a) must be cited for both print and electronic books. For both print and electronic articles, the periodical name and volume, issue, and page numbers (b) must be cited. The database name, database publisher name, and URL (d) are included only when citing electronic sources because these do not apply to print media.

81. B: When students quote others' writing in their research papers, one general principle is if they cannot write the same number of words as/more than in the quotation to analyze, explain, refute, or support that quotation, they are most likely using the quotation as padding to make their papers longer. Another way students often pad papers is by following a quotation with a summary of what it means, which is inadvisable (c) because summarizing it is not as engaging or original intellectually as analyzing, synthesizing, and/or evaluating it (d). It is not true that parenthetically identifying other related studies within a sentence interrupts one's argument (a); this is actually a good technique for incorporating others' work that agrees/disagrees with one's position without disrupting the flow of the writing.

82. B, C, and D: Speechmakers are advised not to be formal (a) or theatrical (e) in their presentation, but rather to be more natural (d) as they would behave in a normal conversation. This makes audiences more comfortable and enables them to relate better to the speaker and the speech. Speakers should also be confident (c), which will support effective speech delivery better than being obviously ill at ease. To establish rapport with the audience, speakers can connect personally with them by being direct (b).

83. A: Experts do advise communications presenters to combine two or three types of media for the most effectiveness, rather than limiting themselves to only one (b). The presenter's budget will also necessarily influence their choice of media (c). For example, TV is more expensive than radio; radio is more expensive than paying a PR writer for print communications; and some presenters can

produce their own news releases and photos at no additional cost. How long a communication is will affect the media choice (d), e.g., in terms of costs and of maintaining audience attention, etc.

84. A: When a speaker is making a statement or answering a question from the audience, s/he should not take three or more minutes to get to the point, which will lose listener attention. Getting off the subject has the same effect. However, speakers should not be afraid to pause before answering audience questions (b): this gives them time to formulate a clear response, as well as demonstrating to their listeners that they are thoughtful and in control. Including too many anecdotes and details (c) is not good: it causes audiences to lose track of the subject/get confused. Similarly, speakers should include necessary information but not all other interesting information. (d): Information overload triggers listeners' brains to shut down due to having more input than they can process.

85. B: Despite that the question is repeated often, this method of appeal is not best identified as repetition (a), but as slogan use. (b): The question which the ads have made familiar is an example of a company/brand's slogan. Slogans are catchphrases that advertisers want consumers to remember and associate with their brands. A bandwagon (c) appeal advises using a brand because everybody else does, i.e., through popularity/peer pressure. A testimonial (d) is a statement endorsing/supporting a brand by a celebrity/well-known individual/other consumer.

86. A = 6, B = 5, C = 4, D = 1, E = 3, F = 2: The song repeating one of the brand name's two words (a) over and over appeals to audiences through repetition. Using words that lack specific meaning but sound good (b), e.g., "best," "tasty," "healthy," "amazing," "smooth and silky," etc., are known as glittering generalities (5). Displaying a brand/product with an American flag (c) appeals by transfer/association (4) of the brand/product with patriotism. Contrasting two brands via a checklist (d), typically with the advertised brand having all features listed against a competing brand having few/none, is a product comparison (1). Showing people in desirable interactions/situations (e) appeals to emotion (3): viewers expect to feel the same by using the product. Citing statistics supporting product efficacy (f) appeals to reason (2).

87. D: Tracing and evaluating arguments and specific claims in a text are shared standards for grades 6 and 7, and delineating and evaluating arguments and specific claims in a text is a standard for grade 8 (a). Distinguishing whether claims are supported by evidence and reasons or not (b) is a part of the standard for grade 6 only. Assessing whether the reasoning in claims is sound and the evidence is relevant and sufficient to support the claims (c) is a part of the standards for grades 7 and 8. Recognizing whether irrelevant evidence has been introduced (d) is a part of the standard for grade 8 only.

88. A = 4: Post hoc ergo propter hoc means after this, therefore because of this. This fallacy assumes that sequence equals causation, i.e., A caused B just because B followed A. b = 1: A straw man fallacy argues against an exaggeration or caricature of someone's argument instead of the real argument. c = 2: Ad hominem means against the man, i.e., arguing against the person making the argument instead of against the argument's validity. d = 3: A non sequitur (Latin for "it does not follow") states a conclusion that does not logically follow the preceding premise. In this example, a missing step is needed, e.g., "Affirmative action will decrease racism."

89. B: When assessing the relevance of any argument, it is important to remember that relevance is a matter of degree, not an either/or or yes/no proposition. In this example, the salesperson's argument for buying the car because of its great paint job is *less* relevant than the transmission's condition (a), which is more important in a good vehicle. The paint job is less relevant than a bent

frame (b), which negatively affects the car's function and value; or how well the engine runs (c), which affects functioning far more than the paint job. However, the paint job is not completely irrelevant (d): most customers want good-looking used cars.

90. D: Teachers should give students learning English as a second language (ESL)/English language learner (ELL) students clear models and examples of what they expect them to do, how to do it, and how the completed results should look. Stating directions verbally alone (a) in English is insufficient for students learning a foreign language. Teachers must also give ELLs more time to respond (b) because it takes them longer to process the English they hear, mentally translate it into their own language, mentally formulate a response in their own language, translate that mentally into English, and judge whether their translation makes sense before they answer. It typically takes ESLs years before they can think in English. When using idioms and figures of speech, teachers should explain these to ELLs (c) and add pantomime demonstrations to help them understand. These expressions are not logical and often have no L1 equivalents for ESLs, so they require explicit instruction.

91. D: Written tests (a) traditionally used to assess learning in native English-speaking students are typically not as effective with ESL students because they do not reveal and may even interfere with ESL student demonstration of what they know and have learned. Oral assessments (b) and/or performance assessments (c) are generally more authentic measures with students learning English.

92. B: It is much more effective to teach ELL students vocabulary within meaningful contexts rather than to teach words in isolation (a). Teachers should limit vocabulary per instructional unit to key words rather than overwhelm ELLs with a large volume (c) of new words. They can gradually increase the numbers of words they teach as ELL student comprehension develops. Teachers should not base ELL reading instruction on ELL levels of speaking English (d), which may be advanced, whereas their English reading fluency may concurrently be at beginning levels.

93. D: When students are unfamiliar with group discussions, teachers should not introduce these by beginning with topics below student age level (a); such topics will bore students and fail to engage them. Neither should teachers assign group discussion topics above student age levels (b), which will confuse, lose, and/or overwhelm them. They should take student cognitive, emotional, behavioral, and social levels of development into account when choosing discussion topics. For all students, and especially those inexperienced with discussion groups, teachers should explain *and* model appropriate behaviors—not just explain (c)—before beginning a discussion. These behaviors include eye contact and confirming and restating others' messages.

94. C: An effective teacher technique for meeting learning goals in classroom discussions if students get off the subject is restating their previous topics and questions. Another good redirection technique is asking new questions about the same topics. To encourage creative and varied student responses, teachers should ask questions instead of making comments (a). When teachers are making comments, it discourages students from doing the same, whereas asking questions invites them to offer different feedback. When some students dominate the discussion, a technique for teachers to engage more reticent students is NOT to ask more challenging questions (b), but *less* challenging questions that can be answered by any student, even unprepared ones. A checklist based on the class attendance roll *is* a good way to assess whether all students are participating (d).

95. A: A PowerPoint presentation is designed as a visual aid to summarize and highlight the main points in a speaker's talk. Slides commonly feature brief verbal phrases/sentences, often numbered

or bulleted, and they also may include pictures, diagrams, graphs, etc. These not only visualize the speaker's main points for audiences, guide listeners through the presentation, and facilitate note taking and outlining by listeners, they also help keep the speaker organized and on the subject. The slides provide an outline of the presentation; the speaker supplies the additional details. A poster (b) is a visual aid, but not a technological tool. It would also not add as much to the presentation as a PowerPoint. A blog (c) and a wiki (d) are both designed for audiences to read online, not read while someone is speaking or listen to someone reading to them aloud.

96. A = 4, B = 5, C = 1, D = 2, E = 3: Edmodo (a) is a social learning platform (4) with resemblances to Facebook that students find familiar, but teachers control it. It includes student and teacher document storage libraries, a shared timeline, a built-in grade book, quizzes, and polls. ScreenR (b) enables teachers to create instructional videos by adding their voice-over recordings to screenshots, i.e., screen casting (5). They can then collate all these videos into a collection (1) on YouTube (c), where students can view them whenever and wherever they choose. WordPress (d) is a blogging platform enabling students to write, post, and read blogs (2). Google Drive (e) is an online storage cloud with built-in Google document programs (3) similar to Microsoft Word, PowerPoint, and Excel.

97. A: In classrooms based on differentiated instruction, the most common differentiation is the way in which individual students access the content they learn because individual student differences often dictate differential means of access. It is common for learning goals to be assessed by standardized testing, which is not differentiated as often (b) except when individual students require alternative assessment. All students in the differentiated classroom should be taught the same concepts (c). The only differentiation is the level of complexity at which concepts are taught, which is individualized. Instructional concepts should not be detailed, but broad and generalized (d) for all students to acquire the same principles and skills.

98. C: Lexile measures assign numbers to many books and articles that identify their reading levels, from below 200L to above 1700L. These are reading levels, NOT grade levels (a). Students can also be assigned Lexile numbers through scores on standardized reading tests they may be given in school. Teachers and students can select texts corresponding to a range around a student's Lexile measure; 50L above and 100L below the student's number is recommended. Lexile measures do not find these texts; teachers and/or students do, and not only texts exactly matching a student's number (b), which would overly restrict available reading material and is unnecessary. Students can generally read and enjoy texts in a range around their level. Lexile measures are not assigned to every book and article published (d); over 80 million articles and over 100,000 books have Lexile measure numbers, providing identification of ample reading matter.

99. A and B: Findings of research into adolescent literacy instruction indicate the strongest support for giving adolescent students explicit instruction in vocabulary (a) and reading comprehension (b). Research also finds support for extended, open student discussion of the texts they are reading (c); for enhancing teen students' motivation for literacy (d); and for enhancing teen students' engagement in literacy (e). All of these have been found to be important by research, but (a) and (b) have been proven the most important of all.

100. C: A good summary of text captures the main ideas in it, omitting the details (a) and other less important information (b). A summary does not literally retell (d) the text or repeat it word for word. It shows reader comprehension by paraphrasing the major meaning of the text in the reader's own words.

101. B, C, and E: Teachers should activate students' existing knowledge (b) to prepare them for reading content; help students determine their purposes for reading (c) before they start; and assess existing student vocabulary knowledge, preteach key text vocabulary, and discuss vocabulary in text (e) students will encounter before they do. They can have students construct graphic organizers (a) *during* reading to help them understand concepts. *After* students read, teachers can have them write about the text and discuss their responses to the text (d) in class.

102. C: According to experts, research shows that teachers should explicitly teach their students writing strategies, including prewriting planning, composition, revision, and editing, by first modeling the strategies; then guiding students in practicing them; and then, once they have learned the strategies, letting students practice using them independently. They should not skip the guided practice step (a): students need assistance learning to apply demonstrated strategies before practicing on their own. Students learn better with than without teacher models (b), which must be presented before, not after guided practice (d).

103. B: Studies show that cooperative learning is an effective practice for teaching many things, including writing (a). Experts recommend that when assigning cooperative writing partners or groups, teachers provide students with both a structure (c), and explicit expectations (d) for both partnership/group and individual performance.

104. C: In the process writing approach, elements include having students write for authentic audiences (a), interact with other students throughout (b) the writing process, take personal responsibility for their written work (c), and self-evaluate their writing (d).

105. A: Formative assessments typically use informal testing methods, whereas summative assessments typically use formal testing methods. Formative assessments typically are not supported statistically (b) or norm referenced as formal, standardized tests are. Unlike summative assessments, formative assessments are made not after (d) but during instruction, enabling teachers to monitor student progress and adjust ongoing instruction as needed.

106. B: Research finds that the single greatest change in classroom instruction for improving student learning and achievement is feedback, which students and teachers get best from formative assessments. Summative assessments are best for comparison (a) of students to normative student samples, classes to statewide/nationwide classes at the same grade level, and schools to other schools, but they do not give such immediate feedback during ongoing instruction (c). Although they yield more individual student data, formative assessments are typically informal and not standardized and hence are not used to make comparisons (d) the way that standardized summative assessments are.

107. A: Critiques of final projects, e.g., art projects, research projects, music recitals, etc., are examples of summative assessments because they measure student achievement following instruction. Oral question-and-answer sessions (b) are examples of formative assessments because they can be brief, can be administered often, and can be used to monitor ongoing student progress. Running records (c) keep track of student performance in real time (e.g., oral reading fluency) and are also formative assessments. Pop quizzes (d) are typically short, may be given at any time, and cover the most recent information during instruction; thus, they are also examples of formative assessments.

108. C: To get data to inform a school improvement plan (a), a teacher could use a summative assessment, comparing student scores at the end of the school year to their baseline scores

obtained at the beginning of that year. This can also be done to show accountability to the federal government (e.g., meeting adequate yearly progress criteria) to get or keep school funding (b); and to get data on student progress toward instructional objectives over the entire school year (d). A teacher would use a formative assessment to get data about individual student performance (c); summative assessments yield more group data and less individual data.

109. C: The acronym K.I.M. in a K.I.M. vocabulary chart stands for key idea, information, and memory clue. Hence, (a) is incorrect. Under the K for key idea, the student enters a vocabulary word (c); hence, (b) is incorrect. Under the I for information, the student enters the definition of the word. Under the M for memory clue, students often make a drawing or attach a picture, sometimes including written/printed captions, to remind them of the word's meaning; hence, (d) is incorrect.

110. D: Having classmates offer peer reviews (a), having the teacher evaluate their work (b), and comparing their work to that of their classmates (c) are all valuable sources of feedback for students about their performance and progress in speaking and enacting through oral reports and presentations as they give different perspectives; however, video recordings of student performance (d) are the only type of completely objective feedback among these choices because they provide an exact record of what the student did. This enables students to self-monitor, make changes/improvements, and appreciate their own progress over time.

Practice Test #2

Practice Questions

1. Which of the following novels was written by Mary Ann Evans under the pen name George Eliot?
    a. *Emma*
    b. *Silas Marner*
    c. *Pride and Prejudice*
    d. *Sense and Sensibility*

2. The historical and social context of Arthur Miller's play *The Crucible* is informed by _____.
    a. The seventeenth-century Salem witch trials
    b. The 1950s Communism "Red Scare"
    c. *The Crucible* is informed by (a) and (b)
    d. *The Crucible* is informed by neither

3. Within the genre of poetry, which subgenre is typically a tripartite poem written to mourn a death?
    a. Epic
    b. Elegy
    c. Epigram
    d. Epistolary

4. Of the following, which is/are true of the haiku but not the limerick as a poetic form? Choose ALL answers that apply.
    a. This form typically is written with a total of 17 syllables.
    b. This form typically is written with a total of five verses.
    c. This form typically is written in an AABBA rhyme scheme.
    d. This form typically captures a nature scene/moment.
    e. This form typically describes a funny and/or silly topic.

5. Which of these is a term that is NOT typically used about a literary dramatic work?
    a. Act
    b. Scene
    c. Stanza
    d. Chapter

6. "A Dialogue of Self and Soul" by William Butler Yeats belongs to which literary genre/subgenre?
    a. Essay
    b. Drama
    c. Poetry
    d. Fiction

7. In which of the following literary forms is the element of literary devices such as similes, metaphors, personification, etc. *most* prominent?
   a. Plays
   b. Poems
   c. Nonfiction
   d. Short stories

8. Which of these literary masterpieces is NOT an epic poem?
   a. Dante's *Divine Comedy*
   b. Milton's *Paradise Lost*
   c. James Joyce's *Ulysses*
   d. Spenser's *The Faerie Queene*

9. Among the following, which element is found exclusively in only one genre of literature?
   a. Plot
   b. Characters
   c. Stage directions
   d. Rhymed/free verse

10. What is true regarding a fundamental contrast between fiction and drama as literary genres? Select ALL correct answers.
    a. Aristotle first defined this contrast between genres.
    b. Plato first articulated this contrast between genres.
    c. Plato first defined it, and Aristotle then developed it.
    d. Fiction did not exist during Plato and Aristotle's day.
    e. What applied to epic then also applies to fiction now.

11. When contrasting the ballad and the sonnet as subgenres of poetry, which of these is accurate?
    a. The ballad is more complex.
    b. The sonnet is more structured.
    c. The ballad is more lyrical.
    d. The sonnet is more narrative.

12. Within the literary genre of poetry, which function is more characteristic of the ballad than the sonnet?
    a. Relating a story about human interactions
    b. Demonstrating skill with writing the poem
    c. Being included as part of theatrical plays
    d. Satirizing romantic, political, and social issues

13. Which of the following characteristics can the fiction subgenres of historical fiction and science fiction be said to share in common?
    a. Both are always about fictional characters.
    b. Both are always about imaginary events.
    c. Both are always speculative in some way.
    d. Both are always closely aligned with facts.

14. According to the ancient Classical definitions, also used by Shakespeare and other playwrights, which of these is NOT necessarily true of the drama subgenres of comedy and tragedy?
    a. Comedy is humorous, and it makes audiences laugh.
    b. Comedy may not be funny, but it has a happy ending.
    c. Tragedy ends in sadness, and it often involves death.
    d. Tragedy inspires terror and pity from the audience.

15. A teacher has students read literary nonfiction by Martin Luther King, Jr. To help them make inferences from text, she does a "think aloud." Text clues are (1) seeing a "White Only" sign made Martin feel sad until he recalled his mother's words and (2) hearing his father's words when preaching made him feel better. Student knowledge is parents make us feel better when we are unhappy. Which of the following would be the most appropriate student *inference*?
    a. Seeing segregation signs in his youth made Martin feel bad.
    b. Martin's feelings and beliefs were influenced by his parents.
    c. When unhappy, Martin felt better due to his parents' words.
    d. When we are unhappy, our parents can make us feel better.

16. Which of the following is the most accurate definition of theme in a work of literature?
    a. A central insight or idea underlying and controlling the work
    b. An author's worldview or revelation expressed in one word
    c. The moral of a story that the author wants to teach readers
    d. The main conflict that was involved in the work of literature

17. Which author writes exclusively from one point of view in the book(s) named?
    a. George R. R. Martin in the series *A Song of Ice and Fire*
    b. J. K. Rowling in her *Harry Potter* series of novels
    c. Barbara Kingsolver in *The Poisonwood Bible*
    d. None of these uses a single point of view

18. One element of literature establishes the emotional climate in a work through the author's choice of setting, details, imagery, objects, and words. One example of this element is mystery. Which of the following is this element?
    a. Tone
    b. Mood
    c. Conflict
    d. Point of view

19. In Kate Chopin's short story "The Story of an Hour" (1894), Chopin's description of Louise Mallard as "...young, with a fair, calm face, whose lines bespoke repression and even a certain strength" contributes to her character development to help explain which plot event most?
    a. Her reaction to seeing her husband alive
    b. The controlling behavior of her husband
    c. Why her immediate grief ended so soon
    d. Her joy when her husband was not dead

Answer the following question based on the excerpt below. Choose ALL correct answers.

Parker surveyed the infield. Ninety feet away at first base, his teammate Jones crouched like a tiger, taking a big lead. Beyond the pitcher at second base, Hernandez slouched a few feet from the bag. Out of the corner of his eye, Parker made out Curtis hopping around at third base. The other team's infielders stood around the infield, staring at Parker, knees bent, waiting to make a play.

Beyond the dirt of the infield paced the outfielders, small, blurry figures in the tall grass. The stands that surrounded the field held a sea of faces. The scoreboard high above the orange fence at straight-away center field, 420 feet from home plate, told the tale: bottom of the ninth inning, two outs, and the home team was down by three runs. Parker held up a sweaty hand to the blue-suited umpire behind the catcher and croaked, "Time."

"Rookie!" someone yelled from the stands.

(McGraw-Hill Education Group)

20. In this passage, which is true of similes, metaphors, and context clues?
    a. "a sea of faces" is a metaphor.
    b. "Jones crouched like a tiger" is a simile.
    c. "Jones crouched like a tiger" is a metaphor.
    d. "taking a big lead" is a context clue to "Jones crouched like a tiger."
    e. "The stands that surrounded the field" is a context clue to "a sea of faces."

21. Through the structure of his poem, "Proem: To the Brooklyn Bridge" (1930), Hart Crane conveys and reinforces senses of _____.
    a. Stability, regularity, and connection
    b. Impermanence, change, insecurity
    c. Irregularity, chaos, and confusion
    d. Eternity free of progress/change

22. Which of the following teacher questions can help students develop the literacy skill of text-to-self connection? Choose ALL correct answers.
    a. How does this book remind you of any other book you have read?
    b. Does anything in the book remind you of anything in your own life?
    c. Are there events in this book similar to events in the real world?
    d. How are some events in this book different from real-life events?
    e. Are there any characters in this book you can relate to personally?

23. What have studies found about how teachers interpret and apply research to reading instruction challenges?
    a. Teachers make data-based instructional decisions better individually than in small groups.
    b. Teachers are generally better at data comprehension than data location in graphs/tables.
    c. Teachers do far better at interpreting relationships among variables than question posing.
    d. Teachers plan differentiated instruction better with real than with hypothetical student scores.

24. The first sentence of *The Bell Jar* by Sylvia Plath is as follows: "It was a queer, sultry summer, the summer they electrocuted the Rosenbergs, and I didn't know what I was doing in New York." What is most accurate about this sentence?
  a. It establishes setting and character elements via literal meaning.
  b. It establishes the symbols to be used throughout in an allegory.
  c. It establishes the setting for a historical novel about the 1950s.
  d. It establishes an extended metaphor using figurative meaning.

Answer the next two questions based on the excerpt below:

> African-American youth are more likely to miss school because they face more barriers to attendance, such as logistical challenges (such as unreliable transportation), school suspension/expulsion or residential instability (consider homelessness or frequent moves). Fortunately, there is an old proverb that guides us to the solution: it takes a village to ensure that all children, especially African-American children, are present in order to learn and develop on a consistent basis.
>
> (Lauren Mims, Fellow, White House Initiative on Educational Excellence, HOMEROOM – official US Department of Education [ED] blog, 10/07/2015)

25. How does this author provide textual evidence of the barriers to attendance she mentions?
  a. She does not provide any evidence of them.
  b. She provides it with parenthetical examples.
  c. She provides it by alluding to an old proverb.
  d. She provides it only by implicit assumptions.

26. Of which barriers to attendance for African-American students does the author offer examples here?
  a. Logistical challenges
  b. Suspension/expulsion
  c. Residential instability
  d. (a) and (c) but not (b)

27. Which element of Herman Melville's novel *Moby-Dick* reflects how he develops the basic, even universal, theme of fate?
  a. Ishmael's multidisciplinary pursuit for whale knowledge
  b. Ahab's attempts to interpret the character of Moby-Dick
  c. Ahab's convincing sailors that his quest is their shared destiny
  d. White sailors' standing/walking upon black slaves/sailors

Answer the next three questions based on the excerpt below.

1. Mamzelle Aurélie possessed a good strong figure, ruddy cheeks, hair that was changing from brown to gray, and a determined eye. She wore a man's hat about the farm and an old blue army overcoat when it was cold, and sometimes top boots.

2. Mamzelle Aurélie had never thought of marrying. She had never been in love. At the age of 20 she had received a proposal, which she had promptly declined, and at the age of 50, she had not yet lived to regret it.

3. So she was quite alone in the world, except for her dog Ponto, and the negroes who lived in her cabins and worked her crops, and the fowls, a few cows, a couple of mules, her gun (with which she shot chicken-hawks), and her religion.

("Regret" by Kate Chopin)

28. Which type of characterization does the author give in the first paragraph?
    a. She makes direct characterization.
    b. She uses indirect characterization.
    c. Direct and indirect characterization
    d. No characterization, just description

29. In the second paragraph, what method of characterization does the author use?
    a. Direct
    b. Indirect
    c. Neither
    d. Both

30. This passage's third paragraph consists of which of these?
    a. A description without any added characterization
    b. Direct characterization throughout that sentence
    c. Mostly description, some indirect characterization
    d. Direct and indirect characterization in equal parts

Answer the next five questions based on the following stanzas from Alfred, Lord Tennyson's

"The Charge of the Light Brigade"

Half a league, half a league,	1
Half a league onward,	2
All in the valley of Death	3
Rode the six hundred.	4
"Forward, the Light Brigade!	5
Charge for the guns!" he said.	6
Into the valley of Death	7
Rode the six hundred.	8
"Forward, the Light Brigade!"	9
Was there a man dismayed?	10
Not though the soldier knew	11
Someone had blundered.	12
Theirs not to make reply,	13
Theirs not to reason why,	14
Theirs but to do and die.	15
Into the valley of Death	16
Rode the six hundred.	17

31. What is the *first* literary device with which Tennyson opens the first stanza above?
   a. Metaphor
   b. Repetition
   c. Hyperbole
   d. Imagery

32. What effect(s) does the poet accomplish with the sound of the first two lines?
   a. Creates a marching rhythm
   b. Makes the distance seem less
   c. Establishes a weary mood
   d. (a) and (c) rather than (b)

33. What is reflected by the word choice of "the valley of Death?"
   a. Allusion to a Biblical psalm
   b. The use of a metaphor
   c. (a) and (b), but not (d)
   d. The use of a simile

34. What are the primary meter and rhyme scheme of the first stanza?
   a. Dactylic dimeter, AABCDDDEC
   b. Iambic pentameter, ABACDCDED
   c. Trochaic tetrameter, AABBCDCDE
   d. Anapestic heptameter, ABACBDDCE

35. How do the form and word choice of lines 13–15 in the second stanza contribute to their meaning?
    a. They reflect the complexity of the battle by using plenty of variety.
    b. They reflect the men's heroic humility and honesty using simplicity.
    c. They reflect the treacherous nature of war by the use of irregularity.
    d. They reflect the tedium of the soldier's life through their monotony.

36. When reading an expository text, the reader would most appropriately draw which kinds of inferences?
    a. Cause and effect and/or problem solution
    b. What events occurred and what people did
    c. What the author wants readers to believe
    d. Ideas that support the author's message

37. In a paired reading strategy for identifying the main idea in informational text, two students silently read a selection. Then, taking two-column notes of main ideas and supporting details, they take turns with the following steps. Which choice sequences these steps in the correct order?
    a. The pair develops main idea consensus / a student paraphrases the main idea / a student explains agreement/disagreement / they take turns finding supporting details.
    b. A student paraphrases the main idea / a student explains agreement/disagreement / the pair develops main idea consensus / they take turns finding supporting details.
    c. They take turns finding supporting details / a student explains agreement/disagreement / a student paraphrases the main idea / the pair develops main idea consensus.
    d. A student explains agreement/disagreement / they take turns finding supporting details / the pair develops main idea consensus / a student paraphrases the main idea.

38. An informational text states that a Yugoslavian nationalist assassinated Austria–Hungary's heir to the throne, Archduke Franz Ferdinand. This triggered a diplomatic crisis in which Austria–Hungary issued the Kingdom of Serbia an ultimatum. In reaction to this ultimatum, a number of previously formed international alliances were then reinforced; therefore, within several weeks, the major world powers had gone to war. Consequently, the fighting soon spread worldwide. This is an example of which kind of structural or organizational pattern?
    a. Descriptive
    b. Cause and effect
    c. Sequence and order
    d. Comparison–contrast

39. Which of the following sentences uses the word "smart" with a negative connotation, rather than a positive connotation or simply the word's denotation?
    a. Eliot's teacher said he was not quite gifted, but too smart for a general class.
    b. Eliot was smart to have studied the day before the test; he got a good grade.
    c. Eliot was identified by his teacher as one of the smart students in her classes.
    d. Eliot got into trouble when he gave a smart answer to his teacher's question.

- 49 -

40. Two groups of students are assigned to compare texts. One group is given speeches by Abraham Lincoln and Stephen Douglas about slavery. The other group is given essays by an author from the Enlightenment and one from the Romantic movement about nature. What are the students most likely to conclude?
    a. Both groups will find that both texts conflict.
    b. One pair of texts will conflict; one will agree.
    c. Both groups will find both texts to be similar.
    d. One pair of texts differs greatly; one differs slightly.

Answer the following question based on the text provided below:

> Cells are our bodies' building blocks. Our body systems contain organs made of tissue, and body tissues are composed of cells. All living organisms, including humans, are made of cells.

41. Of the following questions related to the text above, which one is implicit rather than explicit?
    a. What is the main idea of the text?
    b. Which things are composed of cells?
    c. How do we know birds are made of cells?
    d. What is the role that cells play in our bodies?

42. When reading a research report or other scientific informational text whose author does not overtly state his/her point of view, how can the reader analyze the text to identify the author's purpose and/or point of view?
    a. The reader can consider with what main idea the author seems to want readers to agree.
    b. The reader can consider the author's main point, but examining word choice will not help.
    c. The reader can consider word choice instead of facts/examples affecting reader attitudes.
    d. The reader can consider facts used more than what an author wants to achieve by writing.

43. In the poem "To His Coy Mistress" (~ 1650–1652), Andrew Marvell writes, "The grave's a fine and private place, / But none, I think, do there embrace." Which rhetorical strategy does he employ in these lines?
    a. Satire
    b. Hyperbole
    c. Verbal irony
    d. Understatement

44. As an example of figurative language, who *first* used the "ship of state" metaphor?
    a. Longfellow
    b. Aeschylus
    c. Alcaeus
    d. Plato

45. Of the following criteria for critically evaluating how effective an informational text author's methods of appealing to the reading audience, which is related to whether readers believed the author and why they did or did not?
    a. Clarity
    b. Accuracy
    c. Cohesion
    d. Credibility

46. In the steps that a reader can follow to evaluate an informational text writer's arguments, which should come first?
    a. Identifying the conclusion that the argument makes
    b. Judging the validity/supportiveness of premises
    c. Clarifying premises or reasons with paraphrases
    d. Identifying the supporting premises or reasons

47. In three pieces of informational writing, sample 1's author provides evidence tangential to his argument. Sample 2's author cites anecdotal evidence that is inaccurate. Sample 3's author cites accurate, directly related evidence, but it is an isolated example uncorroborated by any other sources. Which choice correctly matches these samples with incompletely met criteria?
    a. Sample 1's evidence is not sufficient; sample 2's is not relevant; sample 3's is not factual.
    b. Sample 1's evidence is not factual; sample 2's is not sufficient; sample 3's is not relevant.
    c. Sample 1's evidence is not relevant; sample 2's is not factual; sample 3's is not sufficient.
    d. The evidence of samples 1 and 3 is insufficient; sample 2's evidence is factual but irrelevant.

48. A politician supports a point by quoting a statement made by member of the same party. The politician's opponent from the other party refutes the quotation, saying, "Consider the source!" This is an example of using rhetoric to support one's position through which persuasive technique often used in the media?
    a. Ad hominem
    b. Majority belief
    c. Scapegoating
    d. Using denial

49. Which word is a definite article?
    a. A
    b. An
    c. The
    d. None is.

50. "She likes hiking, swimming, rowing, and to climb mountains." Which type of error does this sentence demonstrate?
    a. A run-on sentence
    b. A dangling participle
    c. A sentence fragment
    d. A lack of parallelism

51. Which of the following is mechanically correct?
    a. I saw that the machine did not work because there was a problem with it's motor.
    b. I seen that the machine did not work because there was a problem with its motor.
    c. I saw that the machine did not work because there was a problem with its motor.
    d. I seen that the machine did not work because there was a problem with it's motor.

Answer the next two questions based on the following sentence:

> "Nancy also felt that the party was too crowded, but the hosts, who relied so much on her, would have been hurt if she had not attended."

52. What type of sentence is the sentence above?
    a. Simple
    b. Complex
    c. Compound
    d. Compound–complex

53. In the sentence above, which parts are the independent clauses?
    a. "Nancy also felt…"; "who relied so much on her"
    b. "Nancy also felt…"; "the hosts would have been hurt…"
    c. "who relied so much on her"; "if she had not attended"
    d. "that the party was too crowded"; "who relied so much on her"

54. The syllable *–tion* is a(n) _____ and turns a _____ into a(n) _____.
    a. Suffix; verb; noun
    b. Affix; noun; pronoun
    c. Prefix; noun; verb
    d. Infix; noun; adjective

Answer the next question based on the two sentences below:

> "Don't mind the dog; his bark is worse than his bite."
> "I can tell this tree is an aspen because of its bark."

55. Based on the sentence contexts, which is true about the word *bark*?
    a. It is impossible to tell its meaning because its spelling and pronunciation are the same in both.
    b. The references to the dog in the first sentence and to the tree in the second define its meaning.
    c. "Bark" refers to a sound in the second sentence, and it refers to a plant covering in the first sentence.
    d. The meaning of this word is different in each sentence, but in one of them it is spelled wrong.

56. Edna St. Vincent Millay has written, "Search the fading letters finding / Steadfast in the broken binding / All that once was I!" If the last line were rearranged into more common everyday syntax, how would it read?
    a. All that I was once
    b. Once I was all that.
    c. That I once all was
    d. That all I was once

- 52 -

57. When a middle school student needs to determine whether written sentences in a worksheet are complete and correct for an assignment, which paper or digital reference material should s/he consult?
   a. A paper or a digital encyclopedia
   b. A physical or an online dictionary
   c. A paper or digital grammar guide
   d. A word-processor grammar check

Answer the next question based on the following quotation of dialogue from a novel:

> "Running after t'lads, as usuald!...If I war yah, maister, I'd just slam t'boards i' their faces all on 'em, gentle and simple! Never a day ut yah're off, but yon cat o'Linton comes sneaking hither; and Miss Nelly, shoo's a fine lass!"

58. What kind of dialect is represented in the character's speech?
   a. Early twentieth-century American Southern English
   b. English spoken in eighteenth-century colonial India
   c. English spoken in seventeenth-century rural Scotland
   d. Nineteenth-century Yorkshire working-class dialect

59. "Courage, determination, and perseverance is required for success in this effort." What is grammatically incorrect in this sentence?
   a. There is nothing wrong
   b. Subject-verb agreement
   c. Agreement of verb tense
   d. Lack of parallel structure

60. "He was an old man who fished alone in a skiff in the Gulf Stream and he had gone eighty-four days now without taking a fish" (Ernest Hemingway, *The Old Man and the Sea,* 1953). What type of sentence is this?
   a. A simple sentence
   b. Complex sentence
   c. Compound sentence
   d. Compound–complex

61. What type of sentence includes both independent and dependent clauses?
   a. Complex
   b. Compound
   c. Compound–complex
   d. (a) and (c) but not (b)

62. Which of these versions of the sentence has a compound–complex structure?
   a. She was sick, and so she was not able to attend the party.
   b. She was not able to attend the party because she was sick.
   c. She was feeling sick and was not able to attend the party.
   d. She didn't attend because she was sick; she missed the party.

63. Of the following variations, which one is a simple sentence?
   a. "You could run, but could not hide."
   b. "Although you can run, you can't hide."
   c. "You can run, but you cannot hide."
   d. "Run; run fast, because you can't hide."

64. "He could not finish the test in time even though he tried his hardest." This sentence is of which type?
   a. Compound–complex
   b. Compound
   c. Complex
   d. Simple

65. Linguist Noam Chomsky famously composed the following sentence to prove a point: "Colorless green ideas sleep furiously." What element of language use renders this sentence meaningless?
   a. Incorrect sentence syntax
   b. Contradictory word choice
   c. Lack of proper punctuation
   d. Subject-verb disagreement

66. "To better serve you, we ask that you answer this short survey, it will take less than five minutes." Which common grammatical/mechanical error(s) does this sentence include? Select ALL correct answers.
   a. Inconsistent verb tense
   b. A split infinitive
   c. A comma splice
   d. A misplaced modifier
   e. There are no errors

67. Among seven steps a reader can take to evaluate an author's argument in persuasive writing, which of the first four steps should the reader take *first*?
   a. Evaluate the author's objectivity regarding the issue.
   b. Judge how relevant the supporting evidence provided is.
   c. Identify the author's assumptions regarding the issue.
   d. Identify what supporting evidence the author offers.

68. In explanatory writing, which of the following does the writer typically NOT do?
   a. Differentiate among the members of a given category
   b. Assume some information is factual, accurate, or true
   c. Prove certain information is factual, accurate and true
   d. Define terms, analyze processes, or develop concepts

69. What do the books *Pamela* and *Clarissa* by Richardson, *Dangerous Liaisons* by de Laclos, *The Sorrows of Young Werther* by Goethe, *The History of Emily Montague* by Brooke, and *Frankenstein* by Shelley all have in common?
   a. They are all picaresque novels.
   b. They are all first novels in their countries.
   c. They are all novels written in epistolary form.
   d. They are all novels written in the eighteenth century.

70. To suit their purposes and audiences, which makes blog writing more readable? Choose ALL correct answers.
   a. Avoiding blank spaces within text
   b. Not interrupting text with images
   c. Using all capitals, italics, boldface
   d. Consistently sequencing in posts
   e. Putting text in narrower columns

71. If students in middle school grades are assigned to write text for students in early elementary grades to read, which of the following should they do?
   a. Use script handwriting rather than printing to set examples for the readers.
   b. Use vocabulary, sentence structure, and handwriting on the readers' levels.
   c. Use longer, more complex sentences to provide a challenge for the readers.
   d. Use their usual vocabulary, sentence structure, and handwriting as is natural.

72. When is it most appropriate for students to write in casual language at their own age level?
   a. To share a certain experience with their readers
   b. To get parental permission for a desired activity
   c. To write something for their classmates to read
   d. To write a story that younger children can read

73. Which of the following is accurate regarding paragraph focus and development?
   a. Paragraphs with unrelated sentences are not well developed.
   b. Paragraphs with generalizations but no details are unfocused.
   c. Paragraphs without term definitions or contexts will lack focus.
   d. Paragraphs without needed background are underdeveloped.

74. What structural pattern in a paragraph serves to show readers instead of telling them?
   a. Narration
   b. Description
   c. Classification
   d. Giving examples

75. Among the following transitional words/phrases, which one indicates contrast?
   a. Regardless
   b. Furthermore
   c. Subsequently
   d. It may appear

76. When students are writing the conclusions of their essays, which of these is something they *should* do?
   a. Paraphrase their main thesis statement
   b. Repeat their main thesis statement verbatim
   c. Apologize for their opinions and/or their writing
   d. Always summarize their essay in every conclusion

Copyright © Mometrix Media. You have been licensed one copy of this document for personal use only. Any other reproduction or redistribution is strictly prohibited. All rights reserved.

77. For evaluating the credibility of a source when doing research, which of these is true?
    a. The author's reputation is more important than whether s/he cites sources.
    b. The source should always be as recent as possible, regardless of the subject.
    c. The author's point of view and/or purpose is not germane to the credibility.
    d. The kinds of sources various audiences value influence credibility for them.

78. Among effective research practices, which of the following is most accurate?
    a. If one finds unlimited material, one should broaden one's research question.
    b. If one finds too little related material, one's research question is too narrow.
    c. If one knows the research question first, one can get lost among all the data.
    d. If one finds no existing literature on a new topic, no type of searching helps.

79. Of the following components of a reference citation, which one is needed only for citing electronic sources rather than for both printed and electronic sources?
    a. Author name
    b. Publication date
    c. Book/article title
    d. The date of access

80. Which of the following major style manuals is *most* commonly used for research papers on English literature?
    a. APA style manual
    b. MLA style manual
    c. Chicago style manual
    d. Turabian style manual

81. When incorporating outside sources into a research paper, which of these should students do?
    a. End papers with quotations
    b. Include more brief quotations
    c. Include many longer quotations
    d. Quote only supporting information

82. For making speeches, which nonverbal behaviors enhance audience perceptions of speaker credibility?
    a. Making eye contact with certain listeners
    b. Making random/unrelated body motions
    c. Making startling/novel facial expressions
    d. Making gestures congruent with meaning

83. Of the following attributes of mobile and text media for presenting ideas in public communications, which is a disadvantage?
    a. Popularity
    b. Timeliness
    c. Interactivity
    d. Limited length

84. When comparing digital media to print media, which is/are the greatest digital advantage(s)?
   a. Permanence
   b. (c) and (d)
   c. Versatility
   d. Flexibility

85. An advertisement for a prescription eye drop features a woman identified as a doctor, who both recommends the product to a patient, and she also says she uses it herself with good results. This involves which method(s) of appeal?
   a. Expert opinion
   b. Testimonial
   c. Bandwagon
   d. (a) and (b)

86. Which of the following is an example of a bandwagon method of appeal?
   a. A car is advertised with a beautiful model sitting in it.
   b. A soap ad shows someone bathing under a waterfall.
   c. An ad sings, "Wouldn't you like to be a pepper, too?"
   d. A brand made in USA is shown with an American flag.

87. Among the elements of a written argument, which one do statistics and examples most represent?
   a. Claims
   b. Reasons
   c. Evidence
   d. Counterclaims

88. MATCHING: To assess the soundness of author reasoning, logical fallacies should be identified and negated. Place the number of the Latin term for each logical fallacy in the space next to the letter choice with the statement corresponding to it.
   a. "All great societies have always done it this way." ___   1. *Argumentum ad verecundiam*
   b. "This is true: nobody has ever proven it was false." ___   2. *Argumentum ad populum*
   c. "Drugs are bad, drugs are bad, drugs are bad," etc. ___   3. *Argumentum ad ignorantiam*
   d. "He's a brilliant scientist, so his politics are valid." ___   4. *Argumentum ad nauseam*

89. Suppose a written or spoken argument's claim is that community colleges in your state have recently had their budgets cut. Which of these would be sufficient evidence to prove this claim?
   a. Citing the largest budget cut at one college
   b. Citing two prominent examples of the cuts
   c. Citing examples from 15 of 34 state colleges
   d. Citing specific cut amounts at all 34 colleges

90. What is correct about evidence-based instructional strategies to use with ELL students?
   a. Asking ELL students to explain and/or retell what teachers said to classmates is useful.
   b. To get ELLs to concentrate on language, teachers should avoid incorporating visual aids.
   c. Teachers should not "talk down to" ELLs by presenting abstract ideas in concrete forms.
   d. Teachers may have ELLs signal when they don't understand, but not elaborate verbally.

91. According to research findings, which of these is an example of effective instructional practices to support English language acquisition for ELL students?
    a. Encouraging independence by assigning projects only individually
    b. Writing problems and directions in shorter and simpler sentences
    c. Emphasizing how quickly students finish work, not how accurately
    d. Asking only questions they can answer using lower level cognition

92. The Cognitive Academic Language Learning Approach (CALLA) is found to be helpful for middle school ELL students. What is true of this approach?
    a. It includes content objectives but does not include language objectives.
    b. It includes language objectives but does not include content objectives.
    c. It has content and language objectives, but there are none for learning strategies.
    d. It allows thematically based content or formats using sheltered content.

93. When establishing ground rules for collaborative student discussions, which of these should teachers include?
    a. Teachers should encourage students by allowing them to jump in with comments at any time.
    b. Teachers should encourage talkative students to hold forth to take pressure off of shyer ones.
    c. Teachers should include in student discussions ground rules that students must not engage in cross talk.
    d. Teachers should include rules against verbal abuse, but physical abuse is too unlikely for rules.

94. Which of the following is most accurate about the relationship between the physics of thinking and speaking as they inform classroom instruction in listening actively?
    a. Because thinking outpaces speech, students' minds wander, so listening is less effective than reading.
    b. The disparity between speaking and thinking speeds is conducive to active listening via summarizing.
    c. The process of listening is an inherently social interaction; the process of learning is not equally social.
    d. The process of learning is essentially a reciprocal one, but the process of listening is not as reciprocal.

95. What have research studies found out about the effectiveness of technology-based instructional techniques compared to traditional face-to-face classroom instruction? Choose ALL correct answers.
    a. The majority of studies found better results from blended online and face-to-face instruction.
    b. The majority of studies found better results from traditional face-to-face instruction than online teaching.
    c. The majority of studies found better results from online-only teaching than blended teaching.
    d. One study had better writing from face to face, but there were no comprehension disparities in methods.
    e. One study of two blended courses got better results with an online teacher than in classrooms.

96. A middle school ELA teacher wants to avoid assigning traditional homework wherein students must research a topic and report their findings to the class. Instead, she wants to enable students to make more positive connections by responding to stimuli in a web-based tool as homework, which will also stimulate classroom discussion more effectively. Which technology tool would accomplish this best?
   a. Blog
   b. Podcast
   c. RSS feed
   d. Videoconference

97. Which of the following activities would support a student who is high in Gardner's logical/mathematical intelligence type?
   a. Writing and giving an oral presentation
   b. Designing and using spreadsheets
   c. Composing and performing a song
   d. A cooperative learning project

98. Providing a learning assignment wherein a student is engaged in hands-on activities such as manipulating objects, participating in sports, or dancing would appeal most to which of Gardner's multiple intelligences?
   a. Intrapersonal
   b. Bodily/kinesthetic
   c. Naturalist type
   d. Visual/spatial

99. Among effective reading strategies, which one involves recalling relevant past experience and existing knowledge to construct meaning from the new information in text that one reads?
   a. Inferring
   b. Activating
   c. Questioning
   d. Summarizing

100. In evaluating reading strategies, the US Department of Education's What Works Clearinghouse has reported strong and moderate research evidence for five recommendations of effective practices in teaching adolescent reading. Of these, which ones have strong evidence? Select ALL correct answers.
   a. Instructing students explicitly for learning vocabulary
   b. Explicit, direct instruction in comprehension strategies
   c. Enhancing student interest and involvement in reading
   d. Intensive specialist interventions for struggling readers
   e. Enabling students to discuss text meaning/interpretation

101. According to the Center on Instruction (COI), which of the choices below accurately describes one of several recommendations for teaching adolescent literacy?
   a. Teach effective use of comprehension strategies only in discrete lessons.
   b. Set high standards for text and vocabulary, not questions or conversation.
   c. Focus on student engagement during reading more than motivation to read.
   d. Instruct necessary content knowledge for students' crucial concept mastery.

102. Which element of the process approach to writing is most related to metacognition?
   a. Self-evaluation
   b. Student interactions
   c. Authentic audiences
   d. Personal responsibility

103. When evaluating writing strategies, what does research find about effective instruction of middle school students?
   a. Explicit instruction is best for teaching specific tasks, such as writing argumentative essays.
   b. Explicit instruction is better for teaching brainstorming, editing, or other general processes.
   c. Explicit instruction is necessary to teach specific, general, planning, and compositional tasks.
   d. Explicit instruction is more important to teach revising and editing than planning for writing.

104. If a teacher assigns students to pairs for cooperative writing partnerships, which of the following should their activities include?
   a. One student should write, and the other should review the work.
   b. Each partner in a pair takes turns being the writer and the reviewer.
   c. Each student should provide only positive feedback to the other.
   d. Each student should give only constructive feedback to another.

105. Of the following statements, which is correct about formative and summative assessments?
   a. Summative assessments help students meet learning standards-based goals on time.
   b. Formative assessments allow teachers to adjust instruction to make it more effective.
   c. Summative assessments typically involve students more in the assessment processes.
   d. Formative assessments are more often used for accountability and calculating grades.

106. Which of these is more characteristic of a summative assessment?
   a. The teacher administers it frequently during instruction.
   b. The teacher uses its results to inform teaching changes.
   c. The teacher gives it after lessons, units, or school years are complete.
   d. The teacher relies on it for individualizing student data.

107. Among assessments, which of these is typical of formative ones?
   a. They are most often criterion-referenced tests.
   b. They are most frequently norm-referenced tests.
   c. They are most frequently standardized measures.
   d. They are most often the most objective measures.

108. What approach would be most appropriate for teachers to solicit reflective responses from students about how their ELA curriculum and assessments are designed and used?
   a. Having students take questionnaires
   b. Having students write in journals
   c. Having students rate teachers
   d. Having students write essays

109. A teacher plans to use a rubric to define learning objectives for a class instructional unit, guide students in completing their assignments, and serve as a unit assessment. Which statement is most applicable to incorporating student input into assessment design?
    a. So many premade rubrics are available online, it is unnecessary to "reinvent the wheel."
    b. Only the teacher, who knows learning objectives and how to do it, should create a rubric.
    c. The teacher should collect student input on objectives and assignments to create a rubric.
    d. The students and teacher should all work together in designing the rubric collaboratively.

110. Concerning student self-monitoring strategies in reading, which statement is true?
    a. If students did not comprehend something, they should identify what it is and locate it in the text.
    b. If students did not comprehend something, trying to restate it in their own words will not help.
    c. If students did not comprehend something, reviewing for previous text instances wastes time.
    d. If students did not comprehend something, previewing the text by looking ahead makes it worse.

Constructed Response

1. <u>Textual Interpretation:</u> Based on the following excerpt, write a response that answers the questions following it.

> Most terribly cold it was; it snowed, and was nearly quite dark, and evening-- the last evening of the year. In this cold and darkness there went along the street a poor little girl, bareheaded, and with naked feet. When she left home she had slippers on, it is true; but what was the good of that? They were very large slippers, which her mother had hitherto worn; so large were they; and the poor little thing lost them as she scuffled away across the street, because of two carriages that rolled by dreadfully fast.
>
> One slipper was nowhere to be found; the other had been laid hold of by an urchin, and off he ran with it; he thought it would do capitally for a cradle when he some day or other should have children himself. So the little maiden walked on with her tiny naked feet, that were quite red and blue from cold. She carried a quantity of matches in an old apron, and she held a bundle of them in her hand. Nobody had bought anything of her the whole livelong day; no one had given her a single farthing.
>
> She crept along trembling with cold and hunger--a very picture of sorrow, the poor little thing!
>
> (From "The Little Match Girl" by Hans Christian Andersen)

What is the narrative point of view of the author?

Give specific examples from this text of how Andersen establishes setting, character, and situation.

What kind of mood does these opening paragraphs establish? How does the author create this mood?

2. <u>Teaching Writing:</u> A sixth-grade class had an assignment to write a descriptive essay about a memorable experience during their summer vacation, with their classmates as the audience. The following is an example of one student's essay. Read the essay and then write a response that completes the numbered items following the essay example.

> I have to say the highlight of my summer vacation was our family's trip to Europe. I have never been to any other country before. On this trip we went to several countries. We saw, heard, felt, smelled, and tasted lots of new things.
> First we went to Spain. I got to see the Alhambra in Granada and the Prado Museum and Royal Palace in Madrid.
> Then we went to France. In Paris I got to see the Eiffel Tower, the Arc de Triomphe, and the Louvre. We also went to the French countryside. It was beautiful.
> Then we went to Italy. I got to see the canals in Venice, the Roman Colosseum, the Leaning Tower of Pisa, and the Vatican in Vatican City in Rome.
> Then we went to Germany. I got to see the Brandenburg Gate in Berlin, the Cologne Cathedral in Cologne, and the Heidelberg Castle in Heidelberg.
> I heard different languages in every country. Some people spoke English, but a lot of people did not. Every country had different kinds of food. They also had different kinds of music. They had different customs in different countries. I liked this trip to Europe because so many things there were new and different to me.

1. Identify one strength in this student's writing. Provide several examples of this strength from the text that support your identification. Do NOT include grammar, punctuation, or other writing conventions.

2. Identify one weakness in this student's writing. Provide several examples of this weakness from the text that support your identification. Do NOT include grammar, punctuation, or other writing conventions.

3. Give a description of one follow-up assignment you could give the student of this essay which would either expand upon the strength you identified in #1, OR would remediate the weakness you identified in #2. Explain how this assignment would help the student improve his or her writing.

Answers and Explanations

1. B: Using the pen name of George Eliot, Evans (1819–1880) wrote *Adam Bede, The Mill on the Floss, Silas Marner, Middlemarch,* and other novels. She was very much influenced by her predecessor Jane Austen (1775–1817), who wrote *Emma* (a), *Pride and Prejudice* (c), *Sense and Sensibility* (d), and other novels.

2. C: Both American historical and social contexts of the Salem witch trials in the late 1600s (a) and the fear of communists in the 1950s (b) informed Miller's writing of *The Crucible* (1953). Miller used an overt depiction of the Salem witch trials as an allegory for the panic over Communism he witnessed—and was himself victimized by—during the time he wrote the play. This "Red Scare" was epitomized by McCarthyism, when Senator Joseph McCarthy spearheaded prejudicial investigation and blacklisting of many Americans, including many creative artists, for suspected/accused Communist affiliation/activities. Salem and McCarthyism shared parallel properties of government coercing private citizens to investigate and punish an unproven and ultimately nonexistent "threat." Therefore, (d) is incorrect.

3. B: An elegy is a poem of mourning, traditionally divided into three parts: (1) a lament for the departed, (2) praise of the departed, and (3) solace for the loss of the departed. An epic (a) is a long poem written in stylized language, telling tales of heroic exploits and adventures and combining both dramatic and lyrical conventions. An epigram (c) is a brief poem consisting of one or two lines and using memorable wording to express some wise, perceptive, or witty observation, sentiment, or adage. Epistolary (d) poems are written in the form of letters from one person to another, and they are read as such.

4. A and D: The haiku is typically written with five syllables in the first line, seven in the second, and five in the third. Haiku typically have a total of three lines or verses; limericks typically have five (b). Limericks typically use a regular AABBA rhyme scheme (c); traditional haiku typically do not rhyme. Haiku often capture a scene and/or moment in nature (d). Haiku are typically not humorous or silly, whereas limericks typically are (e)—and they also frequently feature bawdy humor.

5. D: Literary dramatic works, i.e., comedies, tragedies, and other plays, are divided into major sections called acts (a) (even one-act plays have an "act"), and each act is subdivided into scenes (b). Each scene typically is defined by being in a different place and/or time and/or by involving different characters and/or action. Shakespeare and many other playwrights (e.g., ancient Greek, Medieval, Renaissance, Elizabethan, etc.) composed their dramas in poetic verse, so these include stanzas (c), the poetic version of paragraphs. Chapters (d) are divisions not of dramas but of fictional and nonfictional books.

6. C: "A Dialogue of Self and Soul" is a poem. Yeats also wrote a number of masterful essays and a nonfiction book (*A Vision*), but he is most known and lauded for his poetry. This piece is not an essay (a), a subgenre of nonfiction. Despite the word "dialogue" in the title, it is neither a drama (b) nor a novel or other work of fiction (d).

7. B: Poems are the literary forms that most prominently use literary devices such as similes, metaphors, personification, etc. Although authors of plays (a); nonfiction (c) essays, books, etc.; and fictional short stories (d) may certainly use such devices (to varying extents depending on author purpose and style), those literary devices named are most prominently found in poems.

8. C: Dante Alighieri's *Divine Comedy* (*Inferno, Purgatorio,* and *Paradiso*) (a) is an epic poem and a religious allegory. John Milton's *Paradise Lost* (b) is also an epic poem and religious allegory, and so is Edmund Spenser's *The Faerie Queene* (d). However, James Joyce's *Ulysses* (c) is a novel, not a poem. Though Joyce wanted this novel to be an epic, modeled its chapters on adventures of Ulysses (Odysseus) in Homer's epic poem the *Odyssey,* and drew parallels between his characters and Homer's, this book is nevertheless a Modernist novel with elements of realism rather than an epic poem.

9. C: Only the genre of drama includes stage directions, which tell actors where, how, and what they should do physically in plays, which are written to be performed. Plots (a) are found in plays, novels, short stories, and even some poems. Characters (b) are also found in all of these genres. And many plays, particularly early (e.g., ancient Greek; Shakespeare's and other Elizabethan/Renaissance playwrights' work, etc.) as well as some modern and postmodern ones, are written in rhymed and/or free verse (d).

10. B, C, D, and E: A fundamental contrast between fiction and drama is that drama uses direct imitation, i.e., actors portray characters, whereas fiction combines some direct imitation with exposition and narrative. Actually, the concept of fiction (and of fictional extended prose narrative) did not exist during Plato and Aristotle's time (d); however, they contrasted epic versus drama, and the distinctions they made regarding epic works apply equally to fictional works today (e). Plato first defined this contrast (b), and subsequently Aristotle developed it further (c). Hence only (a) is untrue.

11. B: Ballads are less complex than sonnets, not more (a). Sonnets have developed at least five forms: Petrarchan/Italian, Occitan, Shakespearean/English, Spenserian, and Modern are the major ones, but each has its own specific rhyme scheme; all but the Modern have regular meter, and overall, the sonnet form is more structured (b). Although ballads were popularly called "lyrical ballads" in the eighteenth century when they were often set to music, the ballad is actually narrative (c) because it tells a story, whereas the sonnet is lyrical (d) due to its regular rhyme and meter (*sonnet* derives from the Italian *sonetto,* i.e., "little song").

12. A: One major defining characteristic of the ballad is its narrative function. Traditional ballads tell stories of love, jealousy, revenge, murder, etc.; broadside ballads were composed to entertain and inform the common people about current events; literary ballads enabled intellectuals and the socially elite to express themselves artistically. Historical functions of the sonnet include demonstrating one's skill writing in a highly structured poetic form (b); being featured prominently in theatrical plays (c) (some early plays included ballads, but not to the extent of sonnets); and satirizing romantic, political, and social issues of the time (d).

13. C: Although both subgenres are fiction, they are not always about fictional *characters* (a): some tell fictional *stories* about *real* characters—e.g., Anthony Burgess's novel *Nothing Like the Sun* about what he imagined as Shakespeare's life, or Mary Renault's *The Bull from the Sea* about her conception of Theseus (apparently historical figure and myth combined) and the Minotaur. Similarly, other historical and science fiction may contain only fictional characters' fictional individual experiences, but within actual events—e.g., Esther Forbes' novel *Johnny Tremain,* set before and during the American Revolution. Thomas Pynchon's historical novel *Against the Day*; science fiction novels *Earth* by David Brin, *Callahan's Key* by Spider Robinson, *The Astronauts* by Stanislaw Lem; and many others were based on a 1908 explosion (probably from a meteorite or comet) in Tunguska, Siberia. Numerous other examples exist. Some historical and science fiction

- 65 -

works are closely aligned with facts; others are far more imaginative (d). Because they are ultimately fiction, both involve some kind of speculation (c).

14. A: Although the popular modern definition of comedy equates it with humor and making people laugh, this was NOT the ancient Greeks' Classical definition, to which Shakespeare and others also adhered, that comedy may or may not be funny, but it always has a happy ending (b). Ancient Greek, Elizabethan and Renaissance, and modern definitions of tragedy all include sad endings, often involving death (c). According to Aristotle, tragedy should evoke audience emotional responses of terror and pity (d) to be effective.

15. B: Only this choice representing an inference because the students have to draw this conclusion based on clues in the text combined with their own existing knowledge. (a) is not an inference but a clue stated in the text. Choice (c) is also a clue stated in the text. Choice (d) is what the students already know. These choices are the material that the students have from the text and their own background knowledge. Only choice (b) is an inference that they draw based on that material.

16. A: A literary work's theme is a central insight or idea underlying and controlling the work, and it may represent a revelation concerning human nature and/or the author's worldview. It is NOT expressed in only one word (b). It pervades the entire work, controlling author choices about characters, conflict, plot action, and tone; and the work contains evidence to support the theme. It is NOT the moral of a story to be taught (c); morals are explicitly stated in fables, as lessons are stated in parables. However, in fiction, drama, poetry, and other forms of literature, themes are discovered by readers/audiences through the setting, characters, and plot. The theme is NOT the main conflict (d) in the work; it may, however, be related to what the main character learns through resolving that conflict.

17. D: None of these authors writes exclusively from a single point of view in the books named. In the *A Song of Ice and Fire* series, George R. R. Martin (a) alternates writing from different characters' points of view in different chapters. In the *Harry Potter* novels, J. K. Rowling (b) frequently writes third-person limited narrative from Harry Potter's point of view, but also switches to other characters' points of view at times. In her novel *The Poisonwood Bible,* Barbara Kingsolver (c) narrates in the first person, but she sometimes changes to third person for narrating major action scenes in which the first-person narrator is missing or not involved.

18. B: The mood of a literary work establishes the emotional atmosphere through the author's use of setting, details, imagery, objects, and words. One example is a mood of mystery. Tone (a) is the author's implied or stated attitude toward the subject matter of the work. For example, the author might create a humorous, joyous, bitter, ironic, earnest, serious, optimistic, or pessimistic tone through details and word choice. A work's setting or a character might have a mysterious mood, but be treated with a humorous or ironic tone, etc. Conflict (c) is a literary element that provides the basis for a plot. Examples of generalized conflicts include man versus nature, man versus society, man versus man, or man versus self. Point of view (d) is the literary element of who tells the story, e.g., a first-person, third-person objective, third-person limited, or omniscient narrator.

19. C: Chopin's character development of Mrs. Mallard in the quotation includes repression and strength. These explain her not showing shock or denial but weeping immediately upon hearing of her husband's apparent death, but also its short duration: "When the storm of grief had spent itself she went away to her room alone." The quotation does not explain her reaction to seeing her husband alive (a): "heart trouble" previously identified helps explain her heart attack, along with character development indicating relief at freedom from domination (despite love). It does not

- 66 -

explain her husband's behavior (b): another paragraph describing his "powerful will bending hers" explains his controlling nature. The "joy" is NOT at seeing her husband alive (d), which kills her; Louise felt this joy previously upon believing him dead ("'free, free, free!'").

20. A, B, D, and E: "a sea of faces" is a metaphor (a), i.e., it compares two different things without using comparative words (e.g., "like" or "as"), but it implies comparison by referring to faces as a sea. "Jones crouched like a tiger" is a simile (b), i.e., it directly states comparison using "like." "Taking a big lead" is a context clue to "Jones crouched like a tiger" (d), indicating that Jones was preparing to run to and pounce on second base immediately when the batter hit the ball, like a tiger would crouch when preparing to run after and pounce on prey. "The stands that surrounded the field" is a context clue to "a sea of faces" (e): The sentence "The stands that surrounded the field held a sea of faces" indicates the stands held many spectators. This informs the metaphor "a sea of faces," because a sea connotes a large volume. (c) is incorrect: "like a tiger" is a simile, not a metaphor.

21. A: Crane's ode expresses great stability and regularity in a construction that took longer than most people's lifetimes. He conveys how building the bridge persevered regardless of weather, human activity, day or night—even a "bedlamite"'s suicidal jump from it. He does this through structure, e.g., maintaining regular pentameter throughout. Moreover, whenever addressing and/or describing the bridge itself, Crane renders this pentameter even more regular by making it consistently iambic. He even places caesuras (pauses within lines/words) symmetrically (indicated here by spaces between syllables): "And Thee, across the har bor, sil ver-paced /"; "O harp and al tar, of the fur y fused"; or "O Sleep less as the riv er un der thee." Crane also reinforces stability and endurance with frequent alliteration and assonance. Therefore, (b) and (c) are incorrect. Although Crane does portray the bridge as connecting humankind with God ("And of the curveship lend a myth to God") and eternity, (d) is incorrect because he does NOT equate eternity with lack of progress: "All afternoon the cloud-flown derricks turn.../Thy cables breathe the North Atlantic still."

22. B and E: Asking students how a book reminds them of anything in their own lives (b) and whether there are any characters in the book they can relate to personally (e) helps them to make text-to-self connections. Asking students if anything in a book reminds them of any other book they have read (a) is a way of helping them make text-to-text connections. Asking students if events in a book are similar to events in the real world (c) or different from real-life events (d) are ways of helping them make text-to-world connections.

23. D: Research finds that most teachers can plan differentiated instruction based on the findings of studies, and they do this better when using individual scores of real students than with invented scores of hypothetical students. Research has found that teachers make data-based instructional decisions better in small groups than individually, not vice versa (a). Studies show that most teachers can locate data in graphs or tables, but they have more trouble with data comprehension, not vice versa (b). Research also finds that the majority of teachers have difficulty with both interpreting relationships among variables and posing questions (c).

24. A: Plath opens her semiautobiographical novel by establishing the time, place, and main character's feelings of confusion and disaffection through a statement with literal meaning. This book is not an allegory, and the meaning of its first sentence is not symbolic (b). Its nature is closer to a thinly fictionalized memoir than a historical novel (c). The opening sentence quoted does not use figurative meaning, and the novel is not characterized by any overarching extended metaphor (d).

- 67 -

25. B: The author uses examples enclosed in parentheses of the general categories she identifies among barriers to attendance. Both the general categories and parenthetical examples supply textual evidence. Therefore, (a) is incorrect. When she alludes to the old (African) proverb (c), which is "It takes a village to raise a child," she is not providing textual evidence of attendance barriers; her allusion is to support her point about the solution. Since she states categories and examples of barriers explicitly, (d) is also incorrect.

26. D: The author gives an example of logistical challenges (a) as unreliable transportation, and examples of residential instability (c) as homelessness and moving frequently. However, she does not give any examples of suspension or expulsion (b): because being suspended or being expelled is a barrier, examples of these are neither needed nor really possible.

27. C: Melville's development of the basic, even universal, theme of fate—and in this case, how it can be misleading, may not exist, or is ultimately unknowable by humans—is reflected in Ahab's manipulating his crew to believe that his obsessive personal quest for Moby-Dick is also their shared destiny. Ishmael's pursuit for knowledge about whales (a) in an unsuccessful effort to understand Moby-Dick reflects Melville's development of the theme of humankind's finite understanding. Ahab's attempts to interpret Moby-Dick's nature (b) also reflects Melville's development of the same theme, with the whale symbolizing God, whose nature is also humanly unknowable. White sailors' standing/walking on black slaves/sailors (d) reflects Melville's development of the theme of exploitation of indigenous peoples, which whaling shared with unfair trade, buffalo hunting, gold mining, and other elements of white territorial expansionism.

28. B: By describing the character's appearance, the author provides indirect characterization: Her strong figure suggests a strong character; her ruddy cheeks imply vigorous health and personality; her determined eye implies a determined spirit; even her dress suggests an independent woman. Thus, Chopin shows rather than tells readers what Mamzelle Aurélie is like. Telling would be direct characterization (a), (c). Therefore, (d) is incorrect.

29. A: Chopin uses direct characterization in this paragraph by telling readers that the character had never considered marriage, never been in love; declined a proposal years ago, and had not yet lived to regret it. This directly tells readers about this aspect of her character. Indirect (b) characterization would instead show readers about it through the character's actions, thoughts, and/or words, and/or those of other characters. Since (a) is correct and (b) is incorrect, (c) and (d) are also incorrect.

30. C: This paragraph includes mainly description, but there is also a little bit of indirect characterization; thus, (a) is incorrect. The character does not say anything or do much in this paragraph to reveal her character; thus, (b) and (d) are both incorrect. Her having a dog, being religious, and shooting chicken-hawks herself with her gun are elements of indirect characterization. The rest of the paragraph is description establishing setting and situation more than character—i.e., she owned a farm and employed farmhands.

31. B: The first device Tennyson opens with is repetition, of the phrase "Half a league," three times. He uses a metaphor (a) second, in "the valley of Death," an implicit comparison of death to a valley. He does not use hyperbole (c), which is extreme exaggeration for effect, or imagery (d), i.e., descriptions that evoke mental images—visual, auditory, and/or of other senses—as his first device (though "the valley of Death" is a poetic image as well as a metaphor, this is used second, not first).

32. D: The sound of the first two lines creates a rhythm reminiscent of soldiers marching, which is their subject, by repeating dactylic (/ᴗᴗ) and trochaic (/ᴗ) beats. The phrase "half a league" refers to how far they must march (c. 1.5 miles); repeating this does not minimize the distance (b), but emphasizes it as well as establishing the mood of the soldiers' weariness (c).

33. C: The phrase "the valley of Death" not only reminds readers of the Old Testament's Psalm 23 ("The Lord is my shepherd")'s famous line, "Yea, though I walk through the valley of the shadow of death...," (a) it also uses a metaphor (b), i.e., an implicit comparison, of death to a valley, rather than a simile (d), i.e., an explicit comparison (e.g., "death is *like* a valley").

34. A: This stanza uses primarily dactylic (/ᴗᴗ) dimeter (two beats per line). The first two lines rhyme as a couplet (AA); the third and fourth do not (BC); the fifth, sixth, and seventh lines are a rhymed triplet (DDD); the eighth line does not rhyme with others (E); and the ninth line is a near rhyme (aka slant rhyme) with the fourth (C). Iambic pentameter (b) would be five beats per line of (ᴗ /). Trochaic tetrameter (c) would be four beats per line of (/ ᴗ). Anapestic heptameter (d) would be seven beats per line of (ᴗ ᴗ /) (an example is most lines of Poe's "Annabel Lee").

35. B: These lines do not involve a lot of variety (a). Rather, they contain very simple, short words—only two with two syllables, the rest all with one—as well as consistent rhythm. Also, all three lines begin with the same word ("Theirs"), and all three end with rhyming words ("reply, why, die"). This simplicity reflects the meaning that the soldiers do not talk back to their superiors, and do not conjecture about rationales for the battle, but simply do their jobs, which often include dying. These lines are not irregular (c) in rhyme, meter, word choice, word length, etc. Though regular, they are not monotonous (d); in fact, they are some of the most famous, oft-quoted lines from the poem.

36. A: Expository texts are nonfiction works that give information, e.g., how-to instructions or facts about a given subject. Therefore, the most appropriate inferences for the reader to draw would be about cause-and-effect relationships, e.g., in history books, and/or about problems and their solutions. Reader inferences about what events occurred and things people did (b) are more appropriate when reading a nonfictional biography or autobiography. Reader inferences about what the author wants the audience to believe (c) and about ideas that support the author's message (d) are more appropriate when reading persuasive or argumentative text, wherein the author works to convince readers of a position, opinion, or argument.

37. B: In this paired reading strategy, which improves reading comprehension and helps students identify the main idea in informational text, after silently reading a text selection, the pair of students takes turns following these steps: One student paraphrases what s/he thinks the text's main idea is. The other student agrees or disagrees, explaining why. The pair then develops a consensus as to the text's main idea. Then they take turns finding details in the text that support its main idea.

38. B: This is an example of the cause-and-effect structural pattern of informational text because it recounts the events leading up to World War I in a way that suggests how each event led to the next one by using words like "triggered," "in reaction to," "therefore," and "consequently." The descriptive (a) pattern uses sensory imagery enabling readers to see, hear, feel, smell, and taste things; and/or it tells readers the what, who, when, where, and why of the topic. The sequence-and-order (c) pattern arranges events in chronological sequence, or it gives instructions in the order to follow steps. Although this example also relates events in chronological sequence, it is a better example of cause and effect because each successive event is also attributed to the preceding one.

The comparison–contrast (d) pattern identifies the similarities and differences among things or ideas. (A fifth pattern is problem–solution.)

39. D: This use of "smart" has a negative connotation: a "smart" answer here means a disrespectful or impertinent one. This is evident from the sentence context ("Eliot got into trouble"). (a) and (c) use the word "smart" with its literal denotation, meaning intelligent or competent. (b) uses "smart" with a positive connotation, meaning wise or judicious. The context "he got a good grade" informs this use: Eliot was smart to have studied, meaning he used good judgment when he prepared, evidenced by the positive outcome.

40. A: Both groups of students most likely will find both texts conflict in their perspectives on the given topics. Lincoln opposed slavery, Douglas supported it; the two debated this topic while running for president. The Romantic movement was an opposite reaction against the Enlightenment: the latter promoted rationalism, the former emotionalism. Their views of nature differed: Enlightenment thinkers sought to study it objectively, believing they could impose order; Romantics sought to celebrate its chaotic, complex potential, believing they could never completely understand or control it. Hence, both pairs would conflict, not one (b). They would unlikely be similar (c). Neither would differ only slightly (d).

41.C: This question is implicit because the text does not explicitly state anything about birds. However, we can infer that birds are made of cells because the text does explicitly state that all living things are made of cells, and birds are living things. The other choices are all explicit questions because their answers are stated directly in the text (a: Cells are integral to the bodies of all living things; b: organs and tissues; d: the building blocks of our bodies).

42. A: To determine an author's unstated point of view in scientific informational text such as research reports, the reader can analyze the text to discover what main idea the author is communicating, with which the author likely wants readers to agree. The reader can also examine the author's choice of words (b) and how these affect the reader's perceptions of the text subject. The reader should also consider how the author uses facts and/or examples in the text and how these choices affect his or her attitudes (c) toward the topic. Additionally, the reader should consider what he or she thinks the author wanted to accomplish by writing the text (d).

43. D: This is an example of understatement. Using the *carpe diem* tradition as a seduction tactic, Marvell argues that life is short, so we should "seize the day" and make love while we can. In the lines quoted, he understates the condition of death by saying people do not embrace in the grave— when they do not live at all, let alone embrace there. Satire (a) is ridiculing people/groups to expose and criticize their shortcomings. Jonathan Swift wrote biting satires, including *A Tale of a Tub, A Modest Proposal,* and *Gulliver's Travels.* Hyperbole (b) is extreme exaggeration, e.g., "I've told you a million times" or "I have a ton of homework." Verbal irony (c) is using words opposite to their literal meaning: in *Directions to Servants* (1745), Swift wrote, "In Winter Time light the Dining-Room Fire but two Minutes before Dinner is served up, that your Master may see, how saving you are of his Coals."—satirizing servants' habits and lame excuses by presenting them as instructions.

44. C: Alcaeus, lyrical poet of ancient (seventh–sixth century BCE) Greece, was first known to use the metaphor of sailing a ship to represent the government of a city–state or republic. The playwright Aeschylus (sixth–fifth century BCE), known for his tragedies (*The Oresteia, Prometheus Bound*), subsequently used this metaphor in his work *Seven Against Thebes*, also in ancient Greece (b). Thereafter, another very famous ancient Greek philosopher and author Plato (fifth–fourth century BCE) used the same metaphor in his *Republic* (d). In the nineteenth century, English poet

Henry Wadsworth Longfellow (a) used the same figurative meaning as an extended metaphor throughout his 1850 poem, "O Ship of State."

45. D: Credibility is related to how believable readers felt the author's writing was, which is a major element of whether the author's appeals changed the readers' minds, i.e., persuaded them. Clarity (a), another criterion for evaluating methods of appeal, is related to how clearly the author presented the content. Accuracy (b), an additional criterion, is related to whether the content that the author included was factually correct. Cohesion (c), also an evaluative criterion, has to do with how well the author's arguments and appeals are connected and related to one another, which helps readers understand them and holds their interest.

46. A: The first step a reader should take in evaluating the arguments in an informational text is to identify the conclusion the author draws with the argument. The second step is to identify what premises or reasons support this conclusion (d). The third step is to clarify these premises or reasons by paraphrasing them (c) in the reader's own words, which can also show whether the premises fit with the conclusion that they should support. The reader can then list all premises in order, followed by the conclusion, then note any assumptions or premises necessary to support the conclusion that the author may have omitted. The next step is judging whether a deductive reasoning argument is valid or whether an inductive reasoning argument uses true premises that support the conclusion (b).

47. C: Sample 1's author cites evidence that is tangential to his argument; hence, it is not relevant. Sample 2's author cites anecdotal evidence which is inaccurate; hence, it is not factual. Sample 3's author cites evidence which is factual (accurate) and relevant (directly related), but not sufficient (an isolated example uncorroborated by any other sources). Criteria for evaluating evidence used in informational text include that the evidence be relevant, factual, and sufficient to accomplish the author's purpose (e.g., proving the author's point[s] and/or persuading the reader).

48. A: Ad hominem is Latin for "against the man." Another way of describing this tactic is "shooting the messenger." This means the person doing the persuading impugns the message by association with the person delivering it. Examples of the persuasion technique used in the media that involves majority belief (b) are expressions such as "Five million people can't be wrong" or "Four out of five dentists recommend this brand." Scapegoating (c) is blaming one person/group for problems far too complex to attribute to any single individual/group. Using denial (d) is a way to accuse one's opponent without taking responsibility for it, e.g., "I won't mention my opponent's history of legal problems."

49. C: *The* is a definite article because it refers to a specific noun. *A* (a) and *an* (b) are indefinite articles, which refer to nonspecific nouns. For example, "Let's read *a* book" means let's read any book; "Let's read *the* book" means let's read a certain, specified book. Therefore, (d) is incorrect.

50. D: This is an example of nonparallel structure. The first three verbs ("hiking, swimming, rowing") are gerunds (verb participles ending with –*ing*, used as nouns—in this sentence, they are direct objects). Then suddenly the fourth verb ("to climb mountains") is an infinitive. It does not match the others, creating a lack of parallel structure. The sentence should read either "hiking, swimming, rowing, and climbing mountains" or "to hike, to swim, to row, and to climb mountains"/ "to hike, swim, row, and climb mountains."

51. C: First, the past tense of *to see* is *saw,* not *seen. Seen* is the perfect form, used in present perfect, past perfect, and future perfect tenses, e.g., "I have seen," "I had seen," and "I will have seen."

Second, the possessive form of the pronoun *it* is *its*, not *it's*. *It's* is ONLY used as a contraction of *it is*, e.g., "It's raining." An apostrophe is used with possessive proper nouns, e.g., "This is Mary's book," and with possessive nouns, e.g., "This is the teacher's book." However, apostrophes are NOT used with possessive pronouns, e.g., "This is yours," "this is hers," "this is his," or "this is ours."

52. D: This is a compound–complex sentence because it contains two independent clauses plus dependent clauses. A simple (a) sentence is a single independent clause. A complex (b) sentence consists of one independent clause and one dependent clause, e.g., "After she went to the party, she went home." A compound (c) sentence consists of two independent clauses connected by a conjunction, e.g., "She went to the party, and then she went home."

53. B: "Nancy also felt that the party was too crowded" is an independent clause because it has a subject ("Nancy"), verb ("felt") and could stand alone as a complete sentence. "The hosts would have been hurt" is also an independent clause. These two independent clauses are joined by the coordinating conjunction "but." "who relied so much on her" (a), (c), (d) is a dependent clause modifying the subject of the second independent clause, "the hosts". "if she had not attended" (c) is an adjectival dependent clause, introduced by the subordinating conjunction "if" and modifying the predicate "would have been hurt" in the second independent clause. "that the party was too crowded" (d) is an adverbial dependent clause, introduced by the subordinating conjunction "that" and modifying the verb "felt."

54. A: *–tion* is a suffix because it comes at the end of a word. It turns a verb into a noun; e.g., *attend* becomes *attention*; *convert–conversion*; *present–presentation*; *converse–conversation*; *ambulate–ambulation*, etc. Prefixes, suffixes, and infixes are all affixes; however, *-tion* does not turn nouns into pronouns (b). *–tion* does not begin words and hence is not a prefix, and it does not make nouns into verbs (c)—e.g., *fright–frighten*—but vice versa. Infixes come in the middles of words, like *s* in *mothers-in-law* or *passersby*; or in expressions such as "abso-blooming-lutely" in the musical *My Fair Lady*. *–tion* is not an infix and does not make a noun into an adjective (d), e.g., *danger–dangerous*.

55. B: Because "his bark" refers to the dog in the first sentence, the context informs us that here "bark" means the vocal sound that a dog makes. Because "its bark" refers to the aspen tree in the second sentence, the context informs us that here "bark" means the covering of a tree trunk. Hence it is not true that it is impossible to tell the meaning in each sentence despite identical spelling and pronunciation (a). Answer (c) reverses the meanings in the two sentences. The word "bark" is not misspelled in either sentence (d). "Bark" in the first sentence and "bark" in the second sentence are both homonyms—i.e., they sound the same, and they are also homographs—i.e., they are spelled the same, but they have different meanings.

56. A: Millay's meaning, in more ordinary syntax, is "all that I was once" or "all that I once was". She did not mean "Once I was all that" (b), "that I once all was" (c), or "that all I was once" (d). These either mean something different or do not make sense. She makes her syntax more unusual and poetic, first by placing the adverb "once" ahead of the subject and verb and second by reversing the usual order of subject + verb, "I was" to verb + subject, "was I."

57. C: The student should consult a grammar guide to determine whether written sentences are complete and correct. An encyclopedia (a) gives comprehensive information on various content subjects and may include grammatical topics, but it will not explicitly define or explain all rules of syntax and grammar. A dictionary (b) gives the correct spellings, pronunciations, parts of speech, meanings, and origins of vocabulary words rather than grammatical rules. The grammar-check

feature of a word-processor program (d) is a poor choice because its information is incomplete, it lacks human understanding, and its "corrections" are wrong more often than not; moreover, the student would have to type sentences into the word processor for feedback, but he or she could not use it to look up grammar rules.

58. D: This quotation is dialogue spoken by the servant Joseph in the 1847 novel *Wuthering Heights* by Emily Brontë. It is typical of the English spoken by the working class in Yorkshire, the largest county in northern England, during the nineteenth century. People in the American South during the early twentieth century (a) did not speak this way; examples can be found in Harper Lee's novel *To Kill a Mockingbird* (1960), representing Southern American dialect during the 1930s. Colonial Indian English dialects (b) (Babu, Butler/Bearer, Bazaar, Hindi English, etc.) vary widely phonologically, to the extent they are not mutually understandable. None of these sounds like the dialect in the quotation. Despite the word "lass," the quotation represents English, not rural Scottish dialect (c).

59. B: Three nouns are included in the compound subject of this sentence, so the verb should be the plural "are," not the singular "is." There is only one verb, so any error of agreement between/among verb tenses (c) is impossible. Lack of parallel structure (d) involves disagreement among grammatical structures, e.g., "walking, running, and to jump" instead of "walking, running, and jumping." There is no such error in this sentence. Because (b) is correct, (a) is incorrect.

60. C: This is a compound sentence, i.e., one with two independent clauses that could each stand alone as a complete sentence, joined by a coordinating conjunction ("and"). A simple sentence (a) would have only one independent clause, not two. A complex sentence (b) would have an independent clause and a dependent clause. A compound–complex (d) sentence would include at least one dependent clause in addition to the two independent clauses.

61. D: A complex (a) sentence has at least one independent and one dependent clause. A compound (b) sentence has at least two independent clauses, but no dependent clauses. A compound–complex (c) sentence has at least two independent clauses, plus at least one dependent clause.

62. D: Version (a) has a compound structure, i.e., two independent clauses connected by coordinating conjunctions ("and so"). Version (b) has a complex structure, i.e., an independent clause plus a dependent clause ("because she was sick") that could not stand alone as a sentence but depends on the independent clause. Version (c) has a simple sentence structure; the single subject has a compound predicate with two verbs, but it is still only one independent clause. Version (d) is compound–complex, having two independent clauses ("She didn't attend" and "she missed the party") plus one dependent clause ("because she was sick").

63. A: This is a simple sentence, which is a single independent clause (containing a compound verb). Variation (b) is a complex sentence, which has a dependent clause ("Although you can run") that could not be a sentence on its own and depends on the independent clause ("you can't hide"), which could be a sentence by itself. Variation (c) is a compound sentence, which has two independent clauses joined by the coordinating conjunction "but." Variation (d) is a compound–complex sentence that includes two independent clauses ("Run" and "run fast"), each of which could be stand-alone sentences, and a dependent clause ("because you can't hide"), which could not.

64. C: This is a complex sentence. It has one independent clause ("He could not finish the test in time") and a dependent clause ("even though he tried his hardest"), which is subordinate to and depends on the independent clause. It is not a compound–complex (a) sentence, which would have

two independent clauses and at least one dependent clause, because it has only one independent clause. It is not a compound (b) sentence, which has at least two independent clauses but no dependent clauses, because it has only one independent clause and does include a dependent clause. It is not a simple (d) sentence, which would be only one independent clause with no dependent clause.

65. B: Chomsky wrote this sentence to prove the point that correct syntax (a), mechanics (c), and grammar (d) are not enough to produce meaning; semantics (b) must also be correct. The sentence structure and word order are correct in his sentence (a); the period at the end is the only punctuation needed (c); and the verb "sleep" agrees with the plural subject "ideas" (d). However, the adjectives "Colorless" and "green" directly contradict each other: a noun cannot be both; and the adverb "furiously" is incompatible to modify the verb "sleep," which may be done peacefully, quietly, etc. or restlessly, fitfully, etc., but not furiously. Moreover, ideas do not sleep, except metaphorically (e.g., "The latent idea slept in his mind until an experience awakened it.") This sentence provides no context to establish/confirm such a metaphor.

66. B and C: There is no inconsistency of verb tense (a) in this sentence, nor is there any misplaced modifier (d). However, "To better serve you" is a split infinitive (b), which is easily corrected as "to serve you better," and the second comma creates a comma splice (c), i.e., incorrectly separating two independent clauses with a comma instead of the correct punctuation, a semicolon. Therefore, (e) is incorrect.

67. C: The first step the reader should take for evaluating argumentative writing is to identify what assumptions the author has made about the issue s/he discusses in the writing. Assumptions are things that the author accepts without proof. If an author's assumptions are incorrect or illogical, the ensuing argument will be flawed. Readers can be misled by argumentative writing if they do not identify the author's assumptions. The reader's second step is to identify what kinds of evidence the author has offered to support the argument (d). The reader should then take the third step of evaluating how relevant this evidence is (b). The fourth step for the reader is to evaluate how objective the author is about the issue discussed in the writing (a).

68. C: Proving that something is factual, accurate, or true is typically what a writer of argumentative or persuasive writing does. Writers of explanatory writing, in contrast, will assume that something is factual, accurate, and true (b) and then analyze, explain, and clarify this information to help readers understand it. This explanation can include differentiating among members of a given category (a); defining certain terms; analyzing/breaking down processes into their stages, phases, steps, or components; and/or developing concepts (d) for the reading audience. Argumentative writing works to convince readers that something is so; explanatory writing works to explain why something is so.

69. C: The titles named are all epistolary novels, i.e., novels told in the form of series of letters written by their characters. They are not picaresque novels (a), which tell the adventures of a roguish antihero (*pícaro* means "rogue" in Spanish), often humorously and/or satirically. Popular examples include Cervantes' *Don Quixote*, Fielding's *Joseph Andrews* and *Tom Jones*, and Dickens' *Martin Chuzzlewit. The History of Emily Montague* by Frances Brooke (1769) was the first novel written in North America, as well as an epistolary novel, but the others were not first novels in their countries (b). Mary Shelley's *Frankenstein* (1818) was written in the nineteenth century; therefore, not all of these novels were written in the eighteenth century (d).

70. D and E: Bloggers need to be consistent throughout by writing their story or argument sequentially (d) with a beginning, middle, and end because online readers often do not read in order as often as readers of print media with consecutive pages do. Blank spaces within the text should not be avoided (a) but provided regularly, because readers' eyes and brains are taxed by blogs that are too visually busy. For the same reason, text should be broken up by images (b), which are also attention getting and more visually appealing than solid text. Capitals, italics, and boldface should be used only for highlighting, not throughout the text (c). Online paragraphs should be narrower (e) than in print, e.g., 80 characters or fewer (including spaces) to make online reading easier.

71. B: Students should write appropriately to the specific occasion, purpose, and audience to ensure their particular readers will understand what they want to communicate. Therefore, writers in middle school grades should not use more advanced handwriting to set an example for younger readers (a); use longer, more complex sentences to give younger readers a challenge (c); or simply use their own typical levels to make their writing its most natural (d). They should instead use printing, simpler vocabulary and sentence structure, and shorter sentences on the level of readers in the early elementary grades. The primary goal is for the younger readers to understand the writing, so it should be at their reading levels.

72. C: It is most appropriate for students to write using more casual language on their own age level when writing for classmates. This applies whether they are writing narrative, argumentation, exposition, or speculation. When students want to share a particular experience with their readers (a), they should write using descriptive form, rather than persuasive or explanatory form, for example. Age/reading level will be determined by the audience. When students want permission for a desired activity (b), they should write using persuasive form, with mature, serious diction and more sophisticated vocabulary to appeal to parents. To write a story that younger children can read (d), they should write in narrative form, using simpler vocabulary and sentence structure; shorter sentences; more vivid, entertaining word choices; a lighter tone; and humor when appropriate.

73. D: One way writers fail to develop paragraphs sufficiently is omitting necessary background information. Omitting definitions of important terms and/or contexts for others' ideas is another cause of paragraphs that are underdeveloped, rather than lacking focus (c). Descriptions of settings, supporting evidence, and specific details are also necessary for adequate paragraph development. Paragraphs with generalizations but no details are hence undeveloped or underdeveloped, rather than unfocused (b). When the sentences within one paragraph seem unrelated, the paragraph is poorly focused rather than poorly developed (a). Lack of transitions between ideas, and including too many ideas in one paragraph, are additional sources of unfocused/inadequately focused paragraphs.

74. B: The paragraph structural pattern of narration (a) tells readers a story or part of one. The structural pattern of description (b) shows readers instead of telling them. The classification (c) pattern groups individual objects, beings, or ideas into categories by similarity, commonality, or according to an inclusive principle. The pattern of giving examples (d) illustrates points or ideas instead of telling, showing, or grouping them.

75. A: *Regardless* is a transitional word that indicates contrast between the previous idea(s) or point(s) and the following one(s). Others include *nonetheless, even so, however,* etc. *Furthermore* (b) is a transitional word that indicates sequence. Others include *moreover, besides, also, finally,* etc. *Subsequently* (c) is a transitional word indicating time. Others include *thereafter, immediately, previously, simultaneously, so far, presently, since, soon, at last,* etc. *It may appear* (d) is a transitional

phrase indicating concession. Others include *granted that, of course, although it is true that,* etc. Transitions can also indicate place, examples, comparison, cause and effect, repetition, summary, and conclusion. These all enhance coherence by connecting ideas and sentences.

76. A: When students write the concluding paragraphs of their essays and they restate their main thesis, it is better to paraphrase it rather than to repeat the same thesis statement from the essay's introduction word for word (b). Teachers should advise students NOT to apologize for the opinions they expressed or their writing technique (c) in essay conclusions. They should also instruct students that it is NOT necessary for them to use their conclusions to summarize the essay every single time (d).

77. D: To evaluate source credibility, researchers consider not only an author's reputation in the field, but equally whether he or she cites sources (a). These two commonly (but not always) go hand in hand: generally, authors respected in their fields are responsible and cite sources. (In popular fields, some individuals gain favorable reputations without responsible scholarship. This is less common in rigorous academic fields.) In some rapidly changing fields, e.g., information technologies, sources must be current; in others, e.g., nineteenth-century American history (barring new historical discoveries), information published decades ago may still be accurate (b). Researchers must consider author point of view and purpose, which affect neutrality. Sources from certain points of view can be credible but may restrict subject treatment to one side of a debate (c). Audience values influence what they consider credible (d): younger readers accept internet sources more, academics value refereed journals, and local community residents may value mainstream sources such as *Newsweek* magazine.

78. B: If a researcher finds too little material about a research question, he or she should broaden the question, which may be too narrow to yield enough literature. If there is an unmanageable, seemingly unlimited amount of literature, he or she likely needs to narrow, not broaden the research question (a), which is too general. Many people voluntarily doing research enjoy information and can get lost among all the data they find. Knowing the research question in advance can keep the wealth of information from impeding progress (c). On new topics, sometimes no research literature exists yet. This does not mean that no type of searching helps (d): doing systematic searches can help, e.g., first through periodical abstracts to get an overview of literature related to the topic; then through references cited in specific sources like individual research papers and/or references cited in general sources such as books, for specific related topics.

79. D: When citing electronic sources, researchers must include the date they accessed the source in their references. When citing both printed and electronic sources, researchers must include the name of the author (a), the date of publication (b), and the title of the book or article (c).

80. B: The *MLA Style Manual* of the Modern Language Association is most commonly used for research papers on English literature. The *Publication Manual of the American Psychological Association* (APA) (a) is most commonly used for research papers in psychology, sociology, and the other social sciences. *The Chicago Manual of Style* (c) is almost identical to Kate Turabian's style manual (d), entitled *A Manual for Writers of Research Papers, Theses, and Dissertations,* both published by the University of Chicago Press. The only differences are minor modifications addressing the particular needs of students writing papers for courses. Although some instructors prefer and assign Turabian or Chicago style, MLA style is most often preferred for English literature papers.

81. B: Quoting other writers is a good technique for incorporating outside sources into a research paper, but students are advised to keep quotations brief. Longer quotations (c)—e.g., 6–8 long excerpts within a 10-page paper—are excessive. Students sometimes do this to pad their paper length, but they end up with more of others' material than their own. Students should also avoid ending their papers with quotations (a). This can be a ploy to prevent readers from challenging their assertions, to avoid thinking critically and considering multiple alternatives regarding the topic, and/or to avoid writing anything more in their own words about it. Quotations are better used to generate discussion than to suppress it. Students should also quote sources that both support and refute their assertions, not only the former (d). Readers with normal skepticism can more readily agree with writers' positions when they present evidence on both sides of an issue.

82. D: Nonverbal behaviors during speeches influence the listeners' perceptions of the speaker's competence, good character, trustworthiness, and therefore credibility. Speakers should make eye contact with everybody in the audience, not just certain listeners (a). Their body movements should not be random or unrelated (b) to what they are saying (e.g., pacing, face rubbing, playing with one's hair, tapping pencils or toes, etc.), but they should reinforce their verbal messages. Facial expressions should not be startling or unexpected (c); they should be consistent with both the verbal content and the speaker's vocal tones. A speaker's gestures should also be congruent with the meaning (d) of what s/he is saying, to fit with and emphasize the points they are communicating.

83. D: Mobile and text media are very popular (a) and increasingly so, an advantage for effective public communications. Another advantage of text messaging using mobile phones is the timeliness (b) with which information and reminders can be sent. Especially for public communications intended to effect social change, their interactive (c) potential is an additional advantage. Other advantages include decreasing costs and increasing rural reach. One disadvantage of this media format is the limited length (d) to which messages are restricted. However, most presenters work around this disadvantage by inserting hyperlinks to websites/webpages for accessing further information. Other disadvantages include provider charges, although today, more providers are including free texting in mobile plans.

84. B: Although today digital text, images, and sound files can be reliably saved for longer periods of time, digital media are still not necessarily as permanent (a) or long lasting in the same form as text printed on paper, art painted on canvas, or music recorded in some other formats. However, digital media are more versatile (c): they can be displayed globally in multiple locations, on smartphones, palm devices, laptop screens, desktop monitors, giant public video screens, etc. They are more flexible (d): they can be sharpened, blurred, darkened, lightened; parts can be deleted, restored, duplicated, recombined, transposed, etc.; and changed/adapted for students with diverse needs. They can combine text, video, and audio, which print media cannot; enable students with learning challenges to select the most adaptive formats; and allow multimedia interactivity.

85. D: This description involves both an expert opinion (a) because the woman is identified as a doctor who recommends the prescription and a testimonial (b) because this doctor also identifies herself as a satisfied user of the product. It does not involve a bandwagon (c) appeal, which cites use of a brand by a majority of consumers to persuade others to join them.

86. C: The bandwagon method appeals to audiences to use a brand because it is popular, implying popularity indicates quality. Past Dr Pepper® commercials sang, "I'm a pepper, he's a pepper, she's a pepper…. Wouldn't you like to be a pepper, too?" Associating a car with a beautiful model (a), a soap with a waterfall (b), or a USA-made brand with an American flag (d) are all examples of the

transfer method of appeal: viewers transfer the feelings they get from symbols to associated products and (unconsciously/consciously) want the products to get those feelings.

87. C: Statistics cited and examples given most represent evidence that writers supply to support the claims they make in written arguments. Claims (a) are the writer's basic positions regarding the topic. Reasons (b) also support claims as evidence does; however, evidence involves statistics, specific examples, or other facts from different sources that demonstrate the claim's validity, whereas reasons are given by the writer (e.g., for a claim that overusing digital devices causes harm, a reason could be that texting while driving causes accidents). Counterclaims (d) are claims that refute/oppose/contradict given claims.

88. A = 2: Appeal/argument to the public is fallacious by citing public agreement with something, which does not necessarily prove it is right. B = 3: Appeal/argument to ignorance by assuming something true simply because it has never been proven false is fallacious. C = 4: Simply repeating something over and over to the point of nauseating one's audience without any added proof or support is fallacious. D = 1: Appeal/argument to authority is fallacious when someone uses an authority in one field to prove something in an unrelated field in which that authority has no expertise.

89. C: Citing evidence of only one budget cut (a), even though it is the largest, is not sufficient evidence because it does not represent a significant proportion of all community colleges in the state. Similarly, citing only two examples (b), regardless of their prominence, does not represent a significant proportion of the total. Citing examples from 15 of 34 colleges (c) in the state shows that the general claim is true for a significant proportion of community colleges in the state. Citing specific cut amounts at all 34 colleges (d) is beyond sufficient, to the point of excess: reading/listening audiences would likely be so bored by this amount of evidence, it would distract them from accepting the claim.

90. A: Research finds that one helpful instructional strategy for ELL student language acquisition is to have them explain and/or retell what the teacher just said to their classmates. This not only ensures their comprehension, it also gives them practice analyzing the English they hear, restating/paraphrasing English, and communicating to others in spoken English. Teachers *should* incorporate visual aids (b): studies show supplementing verbal input visually helps ELLs understand concepts in subject content areas as they are learning a foreign language. Research finds that students cannot grasp abstract concepts as readily in a foreign language, so teachers *should* give them concrete objects, pictures, etc. to illustrate and demonstrate ideas as students gradually transition from concrete to abstract in a new language (c). Teachers can arrange for ELLs to signal when they don't understand; teachers should also closely observe ELLs, and if they do not indicate/demonstrate understanding, they *should* elaborate (d) by summarizing, paraphrasing, and giving synonyms.

91. B: Research findings show that it helps ELL students for teachers to assign them in pairs, particularly for projects (a), experiments, and reports; to write problems and directions for them using shorter, simpler sentences (b); to emphasize student work accuracy much more than student work speed (c); and to ask ELL students many questions that they must use higher level cognitive processes to answer (d).

92. D: The CALLA is a content-based approach to language instruction that integrates academic learning strategies that students require to participate in mainstream English-speaking classrooms.

It includes objectives for content (a), language (b), and learning strategies (c), and it allows teachers to plan lessons using content based on themes or formats using sheltered content (d).

93. C: Teachers must establish and communicate clear ground rules for students before initiating collaborative classroom discussions. One rule is to prohibit cross talk, which is counterproductive to equitable conversations. Another rule for teachers to set is that students should not interrupt other students when they are speaking (a). An additional good rule is to caution talkative students not to monopolize the conversation (b). Teachers should not only set a ground rule against verbal abuse of classmates, they should additionally set a rule against physical abuse (e.g., shoving, hitting, kicking, biting, etc.), which is not unlikely (d) with younger students and students with behavioral issues.

94. B: Typical speech is roughly 125 words per minute, whereas typical thinking is estimated at roughly 500 words per minute. This natural disparity does not make listening less effective than reading (a). Although the slower rate of speech and the faster rate of thought do allow students' minds to wander, teachers can have students make use of this time by instructing them to mentally summarize the speech they hear as an active listening technique. This enables students to process, consider, and manipulate heard information and make richer, more creative decisions about it. Listening and learning share the common characteristics of being both social (c) and reciprocal (d).

95. A, D, and E: Most research studies have found that blended instruction, which combines online and traditional face-to-face classroom teaching, achieves the best student outcomes. Most studies have *not* found traditional face-to-face instruction superior to online teaching (b), or online-only instruction superior to blended instruction (c). In one study, student writing performance was better from traditional face-to-face instruction; but student oral and written comprehension was not significantly different regardless of the teaching method (d). In another study comparing two courses, both blending face-to-face teaching with web-based activities, students performed better with an online teacher than students with a teacher in classrooms did (e).

96. A: Students can post, read, and comment on blog posts at home and in school, facilitating homework and classroom discussion. Podcasts (b) can stimulate dialogues between their creators and viewers, but as download files, they preclude dynamic interactions such as class discussions. RSS feeds (c) are good for students/teachers to read teachers'/other students' posts, but they are typically unilateral, not permitting interactive discussion online. Videoconference (d) does enable online communication, but only in real time, and content is not easy to retrieve or saved automatically.

97. B: In his multiple intelligences theory, Howard Gardner defines the logical/mathematical intelligence type as the ability to identify symbolic, numerical, and logical forms and patterns. A teacher could support a student high in this intelligence by assigning activities such as designing and using spreadsheets, organizing and analyzing data, and making estimates and predictions. Writing and giving an oral presentation (a) is an activity that would support a student high in Gardner's verbal/linguistic intelligence type, who excels in spoken and written language and verbal communication. Composing and performing a song (c) is an activity that would support a student high in Gardner's musical/rhythmic intelligence, who can appreciate and/or produce music and rhythms. A cooperative learning project (d) is an activity that would support a student high in Gardner's interpersonal intelligence type, who can detect and understand others' emotions and interacts well with others.

98. B: Students high in bodily/kinesthetic intelligence learn best through hands-on activities such as dancing, sports, and using manipulatives. Those high in intrapersonal (a) intelligence excel at being in tune with, understanding, and explaining their own feelings; they learn best through reflective, metacognitive, and independent activities. Those high in the naturalist (c) intelligence type relate to the natural world and can identify and appreciate patterns in nature. They learn best by observing, studying, classifying, and collecting natural objects and/or studying/interacting with animals. Students high in visual/spatial (d) intelligence excel at visual perception and converting three-dimensional reality into two-dimensional media forms. They learn best through drawing, mapping, reading and making graphs and illustrations, and spatial visualization problems.

99. B: Activating is the term experts use to identify the reading strategy whereby the reader activates prior knowledge and applies it to the new information in reading to construct meaning from it. Inferring (a) is a strategy whereby the reader combines what the text states explicitly with what it does not state but implies, and combines these with what s/he already knows to draw inferences. Questioning (c) is the reading strategy whereby the reader engages in "learning dialogues" with the text, author, classmates, and teachers to ask and answer questions about the text. Summarizing (d) is the reading strategy whereby the reader paraphrases/restates what s/he perceives as the text's meaning.

100. A, B, and D: The What Works Clearinghouse (WWC) reports strong research evidence for giving students explicit vocabulary instruction (a) and explicit and direct instruction in reading comprehension strategies (b) and for giving struggling readers intensive, individualized interventions by trained specialists (d). The WWC reports research findings of moderate evidence for getting students more motivated for and engaged in learning reading (c) and for giving students opportunities to engage in extended discussions of text meanings and interpretations (e).

101. D: Research-based recommendations from the COI include teaching students how to use effective reading comprehension strategies—as well as giving them supportive practice in using them—throughout the school day (a); setting and sustaining high standards for text, vocabulary, AND questions and conversation (b); focusing equally on raising student motivation to read and student engagement with reading (c); and instructing students in the content knowledge they need to master concepts crucial to their comprehension and learning (d).

102. A: Metacognition is the ability to "think about thinking," i.e., to reflect on, analyze, and understand one's own thinking processes. Through the process approach to writing, students learn how to evaluate their own writing in more objective and constructive ways. In the process approach, students interact more often and consistently with their peers while writing. This element of student interactions (b) is more related to collaboration and social skills than metacognition. Another element of process writing is the identification of authentic audiences (c): knowing for whom they are writing helps students focus on achieving specific purposes and identifying which kinds of reasoning/logic, tone, and word choice to use to appeal to those audiences. This is more other-oriented than metacognitive/self-oriented. Process writing also includes the element of personal student responsibility for writing (d). Such ownership enables greater independence in student choices, craft, practice, and motivation more than self-analysis of cognitive processes.

103. C: For teaching middle school students effective writing strategies, teachers need to give explicit instruction in specific tasks such as steps in writing argumentative essays (a) and in more general processes such as brainstorming, editing, etc. (b); teachers also should give explicit

instruction in planning before writing and in revising and editing during writing (d). Explicit instruction is equally important to teach effective strategies for all of these.

104. B: When teachers assign cooperative writing partnerships, each student in a pair should not always take only one role (a); they must both take turns writing and reviewing their partner's writing (b) to experience both roles in the process. Each student should provide not only positive feedback (c) or only constructive feedback (d) to a partner, but both. For example, if the assignment is using descriptive adjectives, positive feedback would be identifying specific descriptive adjectives the partner used; constructive feedback could be identifying sentences that could use more descriptive adjectives.

105. B: Because formative assessments are done during learning in progress, they enable a teacher to make changes to his or her instruction via the feedback that the assessment gives them. If one strategy/technique is not working, they can modify it or substitute another one; increase/decrease the pace of procedures, increase/decrease repetitions; change instructional modalities, etc. to tailor instruction to the individual student's learning rates, needs, styles, preferences, and interests to optimize learning. Hence, formative assessments also help students meet learning standards-based goals on time. Summative assessments cannot do this (a) because they are given after instruction is completed and less often, so they do not allow time to change ongoing instruction to expedite progress. Formative assessments typically involve students more in the assessment processes, not summative assessments (c). Summative assessments are more often used to provide accountability and to calculate student grades, not formative assessments (d).

106. C: Summative assessments are administered after instruction and less often than formative assessments, which teachers make more frequently during instruction (a) to inform changes to make their teaching more effective (b). Typical times for summative assessments are after each lesson, unit, and school year is completed (c). Teachers rely on formative, not summative assessments for individual student data (d); they rely on summative assessment results for group data and group comparisons.

107. A: Formative assessments are most often criterion-referenced tests, which measure a student's performance against a predetermined criterion that indicates success or proficiency. They are typically not norm-referenced tests (b), which measure a student's performance against the average performance (scores) of normative sample student groups, such as standardized tests used as summative assessments. Formative assessments may occasionally be standardized, but most frequently they are informal measures (c). They are not the most objective (d)—formal tests are— but formative assessments are better for monitoring student progress, evaluating teacher effectiveness, and informing instructional adjustments.

108. B: Questionnaires (a) typically use short-answer items such as yes/no questions/statements, Likert scales measuring within a range of agreement/disagreement, like/dislike, etc. rather than open-ended requests for reflective comments or feedback. Having students rate teachers (c) is inappropriate because the focus is on curriculum and assessment design and use, not on a teacher's performance. Assigning essays (d) is more likely to obtain students writing about the subject matter itself rather than their reflective responses. Having students write in journals (b) enables them to reflect on their course matter and tests and record these reflections, which teachers can then read.

109. D: Although there are many ready-made rubrics available online free of charge, and a teacher's selecting one this way eliminates added work (a), it does nothing to incorporate student input.

- 81 -

Although the teacher knows the learning objectives and how to create a rubric, the teacher is not the only one who should do it (b): collaborating with students will not only ensure that they know and understand the learning objectives as well as teach them how to design rubrics, but it will also incorporate their input and feedback about curriculum and assessment into the design. Rather than collecting student input and then creating the rubric alone (c), the teacher should work together with all students to incorporate their input (d).

110. A: One self-monitoring strategy to aid reading comprehension is for students to locate the problem by isolating what part of the text they did not understand, which words were difficult, and specifically what did not make sense to them. Another self-monitoring strategy for students is trying to paraphrase the text they had trouble understanding, which often helps (b). An additional strategy is to review the text for earlier instances of the same topic/information the student finds unclear to see if those shed light on the current instance. This can inform reading and is not a waste of time (c). Another self-monitoring strategy is to preview the text so see if explanations, elaboration, illustrations, or other graphics later in the text might clarify what students are currently reading. Looking ahead does not make a comprehension problem worse (d) and sometimes solves it.